Theory and Practice
of
Presswork

This book consists of 37 lectures that introduce the theory and practice of presswork to an apprentice who would have entered into a longer program with the US Government Printing Office. Ocotillo Press has chosen to bring this title back into print for enthusiasts and artisans who may benefit from the content of the book. With the increasing consolidation and automation in the printing field there are fewer opportunities to acquire the knowledge needed to succeed in printing and binding as a small, independent printer.

Should you have suggestions or feedback on ways to improve this book please send email to Books@OcotilloPress.com

Edited 2021 Ocotillo Press
ISBN 978-1-954285-59-0

Ocotillo Press
Houston, TX 77017
Books@OcotilloPress.com

Theory and Practice
of Presswork

United States Government Printing Office

Training Series

ISSUED BY THE PUBLIC PRINTER UNDER AUTHORITY OF
SECTION 51 OF AN ACT OF CONGRESS APPROVED JANUARY 12, 1895
WASHINGTON : 1948
REVISED 1962

UNITED STATES GOVERNMENT PRINTING OFFICE

James L. Harrison, Public Printer

Harry D. Merold, Deputy Public Printer

Felix E. Cristofane, Administrative Assistant to Public Printer

Eustis E. Morsberger, Special Assistant to Public Printer

Milton J. Havener, Director of Personnel

John H. Gruver, Assistant Director of Personnel

Theodore T. Meyers, Chief, Training Section

Frederick W. Baumann, Jr., Planning-Production Manager

Albert O. Luther, Assistant Planning-Production Manager for Production

James W. Tew, Assistant Planning-Production Manager for Planning

Frank H. Mortimer, Assistant Planning-Production Manager for
Typography and Design

Presswork Revisions by Howard W. Amos, Harry A. Estes, George M. Hill,
and Robert W. Colvin

Alfred E. Saki, Supervisor, Apprentice Training, Editor

For sale by the Superintendent of Documents, U.S. Government Printing Office
Washington 25, D.C. - Price $1.75

Preface

THE UNITED STATES GOVERNMENT PRINTING OFFICE is authorized by law to conduct a training program for apprentices in the various graphic-arts trades. As a part of its Division of Personnel, the Office maintains a Training Section where a staff and special lecturers provide instruction and training in the theory and practice of the printing arts. This classroom training complements the on-the-job instruction and work experience which each apprentice receives in the production divisions of the Government Printing Office.

The term of apprenticeship is 5 years.

Training begins with an indoctrination period. Each apprentice is given a broad view of the graphic arts, with rotating work assignments in all the various production divisions. This provides the student and his supervisors and instructors an opportunity to weigh aptitudes and preferences before assignments are made to specialized fields.

On completion of the rotation through production sections, assignments to crafts are made and specialized trade training commences. Each production section has a training representative whose function is to demonstrate and teach the processes of that section.

Some special trade texts are utilized and there are six pre-planned courses which are compulsory for all apprentices. Two of these courses, "History of Printing" and "Practical English and Effective Speech," include regular examinations as well as detailed lectures. "Organization of the United States Government," "United States Government Printing Office Style Manual," "Planning and Estimating," and "Administrative Responsibilities of the Office" are lecture courses.

Eight division heads, the Superintendent of Documents, the Plant Engineer, the Director of Purchases, the Technical Director, the Planning-Production Manager, the Comptroller, the Assistant Planning-Production Manager for Typography and Design, and the Director of Personnel, and their supervisory staffs combine to present the lectures on "Administrative Responsibilities of the Office." The result is a comprehensive functional instruction and analysis of the Government Printing Office and its relationship to the Congress and other Federal agencies.

After the satisfactory completion of the 5-year program, the apprentices are graduated as journeymen in their chosen field. The success of this program of intensive classroom and on-the-job training, coupled with rotating production assignments leading to a final specialization, is attested by the fact that many graduates of the program hold key positions throughout the Government Printing Office. Some now are holding important graphic-arts positions with the Congress and in other Government agencies, and a few left the public service to serve with distinction in private enterprise.

JAMES L. HARRISON,
Public Printer.

GOVERNMENT PRINTING OFFICE
Washington, D.C.

Contents

	Page
PREFACE.	iii–iv

1. PRESSWORK AS A VOCATION 1

Three classes of presswork. Variety of equipment. Advantages. Qualifications of a pressman.

2. APPRENTICE PRESSMAN 5

Rules and methods of procedure. Interest in work. Direct supervision. Carefulness. Origin of printing. Principal materials essential to presswork.

3. PRINTING PROCESSES AND PRINTING MEDIA 11

Letterpress process. Planographic process. Intaglio process.

4. PRESS CONTROLS AND SAFETY 17

Three safety factors. Early printing presses. Later improvements. Belt-driven power machinery. Direct-drive electric-power machinery. Two general groups of machines. Control of speed. Power controls. Mechanical controls. When and how to start presses. Stopping the press. Mechanical trip devices. Caution in operating electrical switches.

5. LETTERPRESS PRINTING MACHINES 25

Inking unit. Printing unit. Feeding unit. Delivery unit.

6. PRESS SECTIONS IN THE LETTERPRESS DIVISION 33

a. Main Press Section. Emergency, Web, Job, Book, Illustration. b. Postal Card.

7. EQUIPMENT FOR PRESSWORK 37

Pressman's individual equipment. Office tools and equipment. Maintenance Division.

8. CLEANING PRESSROOM EQUIPMENT 43

Reasons equipment should be kept clean. Cleaning preparations used in the pressroom. Methods of cleaning equipment. Safety precautions.

Page

9. THE DEVELOPMENT OF PLATEN PRESSES............. 47

Platen press defined. The first recorded use of the printing press. Notable names in the development of the platen press.

10. THE DEVELOPMENT OF CYLINDER PRESSES......... 53

Letterpress machines. Some notable names in the development of cylinder presses.

11. THE DEVELOPMENT OF ROTARY PRESSES.......... 59

Some notable names in the development of rotary presses. Important uses of web presses.

12. PREPARING TYPE FORMS FOR PRESS.............. 65

Two principal kinds of type forms. Precautions to be observed when preparing type forms.

13. PLACING TYPE FORMS ON THE PRESS............. 71

Placing type forms on platen presses. Placing type forms on vertical presses. Placing type forms on cylinder presses. Safety precautions.

14. PRESS IMPOSITION OF PLATE FORMS................ 77

Factors to be considered before imposing plates. Method of positioning plates. Importance of guide marker.

15. PRINTING INKS............................. 81

History of printing inks. Definition of term "Printing Inks." Manufacture of ink. Raw materials. Types of printing inks.

16. ROLLERS FOR PRINTING PRESSES................ 93

History. Ingredients. Manufacture.

17. THE SETTING AND CARE OF ROLLERS............. 99

Two kinds of inking mechanisms for cylinder presses. Setting cylinder-press rollers. Setting platen-press rollers. Marking rollers. Caring for rollers.

18. PAPER.................................... 105

Early writing material. Invention and development of paper. Fourdrinier papermaking machine. Wood pulp. Rag pulp. Common terms used in connection with paper. Kinds of paper generally used in the pressroom. Three outstanding characteristics of paper.

Page

19. PLATEN PRESSES........................... 111

Press mechanism, operation and care of platen presses.

20. PACKING VERTICAL PRESSES................... 119

Review press controls. Prepare the press. Remove feed-board. Remove old packing. Apply new packing. Observe safety precautions.

21. PACKING CYLINDER PRESSES.................. 125

Removing old packings. Cleaning cylinder. Preparing new packings. Hanging new packings.

22. WHY IS MAKEREADY NECESSARY?............... 131

Theory of letterpress printing. Four main factors which necessitate regulation of pressure. Printing without make-ready.

23. MAKEREADY FUNDAMENTALS.................. 137

Factors which influence the amount of makeready. Preparing the form. Making press adjustments. Regulating the impression. Marking out the sheet. Patching the sheet. Hanging the makeready or overlay sheet.

24. MAKEREADY UNDERLAY AND INTERLAY.......... 143

Definition of underlay and interlay. Underlay. Interlay. Plugging quoins. Advantages of underlay and interlay.

25. MAKEREADY OVERLAY....................... 149

Definition of overlay. The pitch line. The sheet to be used for overlay. Important things to remember.

26. MECHANISM OF CYLINDER PRESSES—FEEDING UNIT.. 155

The feedboard. Front guides. Grippers. Bands. Brush. Manila apron.

27. MECHANISM OF CYLINDER PRESSES—PRINTING UNIT. 161

Power control. Foot pedals. Printing unit.

28. MECHANISM OF CYLINDER PRESSES—FEEDER AND DELIVERY UNITS............................ 167

29. MAKEREADY FOR CYLINDER PRESSES............. 173

Packing cylinder. Positioning sheet. Cleaning press parts. Positioning form on bed of press. Locking chase on bed of press. Positioning rollers. Inking the press. Pulling sheet to check position. Marking out interlay. Hanging overlay.

Page

30. The Care and Operation of Cylinder Presses....   179

Care of the press. The press run.

31. The Adjustment of Kluge Feeders............   185

To accommodate various kinds of stock. To prepare for make-
ready. To set feeder for press run. To set delivery arm. To
adjust the feeding magazine. To load the feeding magazine.
To provide the blast to separate the sheets. To run the feeder.
To set the jogger. Things to remember while operating the
Kluge feeder.

32. The Mechanism of Miehle Vertical Presses.....   193

Advantages. Mechanism. Frames. Installation. Driving
mechanism. Stop cylinder. Cylinder trip. Outstanding
features.

33. Printing Illustrations........................   199

Three methods of printing pictures. Wood cuts. Line cuts
or zinc etchings. The benday process. Halftones.

34. Web Presses................................   205

Kinds of web presses in GPO. Principal components of a web
press. Operating and making ready. Trouble hints.

35. Time Reporting.............................   213

Reasons for modern accounting system. Basic cards for the
trainee. Electronic data processing.

36. Modernization.............................   217

Wrap-around. Dycril. Heidelberg.

37. Concluding Remarks........................   219

CHAPTER 1

Presswork as a Vocation

SUBJECT OUTLINE

A. Three classes of presswork.
B. Variety of equipment.
C. Advantages.
D. Qualifications of a pressman:
    1. Physical requirements:
        a. Ability to lift.
        b. Coordination.
        c. Good eyesight.
        d. Agility.
        e. Good hearing.
        f. Steady nerves.
        g. Sense of equilibrium.

2. Temperament:
    a. Readiness to accept advice.
    b. Mental alertness.
    c. Good judgment.
3. Other important considerations:
    a. Common sense.
    b. Mechanical ability.
    c. Knowledge of mathematics, paper, inks, and static electricity.
    d. Exercise of care.
    e. Adequate supply of tools.

From its crude beginnings the printing industry has developed into highly specialized branches which may be classified in three general groups: composition, presswork, and bindery operations. Presswork may be further divided into three classes: letterpress, lithographic, and gravure printing, each of which requires equipment and procedures too numerous to consider at this time.

Presswork is the actual production branch of the printing trade. It is in the pressroom that the output of some of the other allied printing branches is assembled and transformed into the readable product. Paper, ink, type, plates, and many other items are brought together on the press, where the actual work of printing is done.

Perhaps the Government Printing Office has a greater variety of letterpress machines than any other printing establishment. These presses vary in size from those only a little larger than a typewriter, to the large Record presses, which are similar to those used to print newspapers. It is planned to acquaint the apprentices with this array of machinery as rapidly as possible.

With such a variety of equipment, it may be seen that presswork cannot be monotonous. It would not be very difficult to train an apprentice as a specialist in the operation of any one of these machines, but it is the purpose of the Government Printing Office Training Section to prepare journeymen who will be able to work efficiently with all of them.

Certain **advantages** are enjoyed by pressmen in the Government Printing Office. The pressrooms are air-conditioned, with a year-around temperature of 74°. Although the air-conditioning system was installed primarily to improve printing conditions, the workers in the pressroom also enjoy its benefits. In the old Book and Record Sections of the pressroom, the temperature was sometimes as high as 115°, and salt tablets were provided and taken regularly by the workers. Although cooling fans were used directly on the rollers, conditions at times were almost unbearable, and roller trouble was frequently experienced. This difficulty has been remedied by the even temperature provided by the air-conditioning system.

Since pressmen work indoors, they enjoy year-around employment with no necessity to lose time because of inclement weather. The pay is good as pressmen are among the highest paid mechanics, and there is extra financial compensation for those attaining the position of head pressmen on certain machines. Vacations with pay and sick-leave benefits are provided throughout the Office. The work is interesting, since each job is different, presenting new problems.

Presswork is not laborious. Although a pressman may work steadily while making ready or preparing for the press run, he may be able to relax to a certain extent while the press is running, although it must always be remembered that a printing press requires constant watching while it is running.

In discussing the **qualifications** of a pressman, we consider first the **physical requirements**. He should have the **ability to lift**, as he is required to move large type forms and patent bases to the bed of the press; to remove, load, and unload large lots of paper; and to handle heavy plates, etc. But this kind of lifting is not strenuous enough to require extraordinary strength, and heavy work is infrequent and of short duration.

Another important qualification is the **ability to coordinate** the mind and hand. In the various press operations which include laying plates, handling type forms, cutting overlays, using tools to make adjustments, and in hand feeding the presses, etc., coordination is very important.

Naturally **good eyesight** or properly corrected vision is another requisite. The pressman uses his eyes constantly on close work. He should possess fine color perception, an understanding of color harmony, and the ability to tell at a glance the proper distribution of the ink on the sheet. Color blindness is a definite handicap. Many of the eye troubles of the pressmen have been remedied through improved lighting of the pressrooms.

There is also need for **agility** on the part of the pressman. The operation of some of the larger presses requires that he do much climbing while making ready and during the press run. His **hearing** should be sufficiently good to detect any change in the normal running sound of the presses. He requires **steady nerves** and a **sense of equilibrium** to work in the clamor of sound and the whirl of fast-moving machinery. As in all indoor jobs, the workman should get plenty of fresh air and outdoor exercise during his leisure hours.

These physical requirements are not too strict, and anyone of average health and strength should be able to qualify. However, some qualifications of **temperament** also are essential in a pressman. He should be **ready to accept advice, mentally alert,** and show **good judgment.**

Besides the physical and temperamental qualities already discussed, there are **other important considerations.** Formal education is not so important as **common sense** and **mechanical ability.** This does not mean that an educated person would be unhappy doing presswork. On the contrary, an educated, intelligent man will find many opportunities to suggest improvements in the operation of the pressroom. A little attention to the various jobs being printed may provide an education in itself. The pressman should not neglect his press duties to improve his mind, but much useful information may be gathered while the presses are running.

Some **knowledge of mathematics** is necessary. The pressman should be familiar with common fractions, decimals, and the measurement of the simpler plane surfaces, squares, circles, diameters, etc. He should be able to grasp the mechanical principles of the action of cams, levers, gears, and screws. Accuracy and speed are required in making press settings and in adjusting cylinders, rollers, stops, guides, grippers, etc. It is important that the pressman know how to use the micrometer and other measuring devices. He should be capable of figuring the measure of type pages, the imposition of forms, the quantity of stock required, the thickness of packing, the printers' point system, and other similar pressroom mathematical problems.

All pressmen should have some **knowledge of the different grades of paper** and how it is manufactured; the chemical properties of **inks** and their making and mixing; and the causes of **static electricity** and how to minimize its effects as much as possible in printing.

It is necessary that the pressman **exercise care in all his work.** Carelessness, whether it arises from overconfidence or from lack of interest, cannot be tolerated. Despite the many **mechanical safe-**

guards in use and the constant improvements being made, accidents will occur, and there is no doubt that many of them could be avoided. Carelessness is inexcusable in a pressman who works around moving machinery.

Presswork is not a white-collar job. It is sometimes dirty and greasy. Special hand soap is needed and must be used many times a day. However, the interesting features of the work compensate for the undesirable. For work on some of the smaller machines, ordinary street clothes may be worn; but work on the larger machines requires special work clothes or overalls. Unless these presses are cleaned regularly, working on them may become an uncomfortable procedure. A pair of shoes should be kept especially for use during work hours, as shoes worn at work will damage rugs and floors if worn at home.

An adequate supply of working tools is essential, and it is necessary for the trainee to provide his own.

In summing up, anyone who really likes mechanical work and has the qualifications mentioned will be happy to make presswork his career. Constant changes, new problems, and special requirements must be faced every day. The field is open for anyone with foresight who is interested in producing better methods of printing. Improvements are being made constantly, and pressmen with initiative have been responsible for many of them. Presswork is an art, not a repetitious performance to be slavishly followed day after day.

QUESTIONS FOR STUDY AND DISCUSSION

1. Into what three groups may the general work of printing be divided?

2. What are the three principal classes of presswork?

3. Discuss some of the advantages enjoyed by pressmen in the Government Printing Office.

4. What are some of the physical qualities necessary in a successful pressman?

5. What characteristics of temperament does a pressman need?

6. What are some other important considerations?

7. Why is a knowledge of mathematics essential? of inks? of the effects of static electricity?

8. What qualification is absolutely necessary if accidents are to be minimized?

9. How would you sum up the advantages of presswork as a vocation?

CHAPTER 2

Apprentice Pressmen

SUBJECT OUTLINE

A. Rules and methods of procedure.
B. Interest in work.
C. Direct supervision.
D. Carefulness.
E. Origin of printing.

F. Principal materials essential to press-work:
1. Paper.
2. Ink.
3. Rollers.
4. The form.
5. The printing press.

In the Government Printing Office and in the Training Section, apprentices will work with men who have had experience in a variety of printing plants. In all commercial printing plants, as well as in the Government Printing Office, definite **rules and methods of procedure** must be followed. These methods may vary in different establishments, and even in different sections of the same plant. When so many new machines, materials, and processes are being introduced continually, it may be readily understood that the rules and procedures must be flexible to meet the constant changes.

During the apprentice training of pressmen, instruction will be given in the methods which have been found to be most practical; also in certain tricks of the trade, and how to meet emergencies. These instructions will apply to the handling of average jobs, and also jobs that are more complicated.

In presswork, we must print from many kinds of forms, use many kinds of ink, and apply impressions to many different kinds of paper. These procedures are further complicated by the variety of presses on which the work is performed. Part of the secret of good printing is the ability to locate trouble and apply the proper remedy. This will be a gradual development as skill in the trade is acquired.

It is of primary importance that the apprentice be **interested** in presswork if he is to make satisfactory progress. By study, observation, and the application of the knowledge he gains, he will soon find that

5

he can handle any work he may be called upon to perform. Throughout this training period there will be many discussions on the theory of presswork which will be beneficial, but the application of the theory will be even more important, since experience is the best teacher.

For some time in the pressroom the apprentice will be allowed to work only under **direct supervision.** He may be called upon to care for rollers, oil the press, handle paper, spot up marked-out, makeready sheets, and in general assist other more experienced men. Then he may begin to apply the knowledge he has gained.

Various pressmen use different methods to accomplish the end results of completing a printed sheet.

Observe the methods and work along with each individual assigned as instructor. Evaluate all procedures and use those that you feel are best when you are working alone.

Before an apprentice is ready to perform the actual work of printing, he will first be assigned the minor duties of a pressman. These minor duties and operations at times may be monotonous and tiring, and progress may seem slow, but they must become second nature to the apprentice before he is allowed to proceed to more complicated work. When he has mastered the simpler tasks and has learned to perform them efficiently, more responsibility will inevitably follow.

Carefulness is one of the most essential qualities in a pressman, and it must be practiced by the apprentice from the very beginning. In the pressroom the results of carelessness are unnecessary waste and serious accidents. In the early stages of training, do not concentrate on speed, for that will come as a gradual development. A better quality and a greater quantity of work will be produced by the exercise of care than in any other way.

Since carefulness must become a habit, it must be exercised from the very start of your training. One act of carelessness may result in permanent disfigurement; and even if it does not result in personal injury, the job may be spoiled or the machine damaged. Troubles in the pressroom occur often enough without the aid of carelessness on the part of the operator.

When a pressman goes about his work from day to day with a minimum of trouble, it is probably due to the fact that he is more careful in everything he does, and knows how to forestall or remedy troubles with a minimum of effort. When troubles which cannot be overcome immediately present themselves, do not hesitate to ask assistance of an experienced pressman. Learn to remedy and overcome difficulties as easily as possible, either by your own initiative or with assistance from others.

Little is known of the **origin of printing**, but we do know that impressions were made by the Chinese from crudely engraved wooden blocks as early as the ninth century. From this obscure start, printing has grown in importance until it now ranks high among the Nation's industries. Printing consists of impressing ink upon paper to convey a message; and though the methods of depositing the ink upon the paper vary, the process is generally known as presswork. If there were no presswork with which to assemble the paper and ink, there would be no printing. Presswork is the hub of the printing craft, the other allied printing branches being chiefly the preparers of material for the pressman.

Several **principal materials are essential to presswork**: paper, ink, rollers, the form, and the press itself. Long ago the ancient Egyptians soaked strips of papyrus in water, and pressed them into thin layers between flat rocks in the sun. The dried residuum constituted the world's first supply of **paper**. Today the same principle, refined and improved and with a wider range of raw material, is used in the manufacture of pulp paper. The sulfite and caustic soda processes are other methods employed in making paper, each producing a different kind.

During the journey of the paper through the mill, it may be subjected to other processes such as calendering, sizing, laiding, coloring, etc. In processing the finer grades of paper, about 60 analyzed chemicals may be used. If substitutions are made of inferior chemicals, or if impure water is used, the affinity of paper for certain printing inks may be totally lost. The utmost care is necessary in the manufacture of paper in sheets of correct surface, uniform thickness, and standardized ingredients, since paper is the largest single factor in printing, and hence vitally important to the pressman.

Unlike paper, **ink** may be changed to suit conditions, and the method of application may vary. The first printing ink of which we have record was made of "well-aged linseed oil boiled until viscous when cold, and mixed in a mortar with resin black." From this small beginning, the enormous printing-ink industry of today has developed. Experienced chemists and inkmakers produce uniform, dependable, workable ink. Some jobs require acidproof ink; some, greaseproof ink; some, copying ink which is easily affected by moisture; and some, double-toned inks which present the appearance of having been printed twice, each time in a different color.

For hundreds of years, ink was distributed over the surface of the form by means of "ink balls" made of untanned sheepskin, stuffed usually with wool. Then leather **rollers** were used, and in 1810 rollers were made of a glue-and-molasses mixture. At the present time, they are usually made principally of glue and glycerin.

"Rollers are to the pressman what brushes are to the artist; they are the tools with which he lays on his colors." They are formed so accurately by the rollermakers that the pressman can adjust them to insure uniform pressure on all parts of the form. He readjusts them as changes occur, and coats them with oil before storing to prevent them from drying out.

Rollers are made several days before they are put into actual use, so that they may be properly aged or seasoned, with enough suction to lift the printing ink from one place to another, sufficient elasticity to conform to depressions or elevations in the form, and yet sufficient toughness to resist melting when subjected to the frictional pull of ink for hours at a stretch.

The message to be printed is prepared and collected in the composing room and delivered to the pressman as a **form**. Forms may be composed of type metal, copper, zinc, nickel, brass, wood, linoleum, steel, rubber, or any combination of these. The manufacturers of these parts all strive for uniformity of product so that the form may be justified accurately enough to be for all practical purposes a unit, thus enabling the pressman to start the actual printing as quickly as possible.

In 1450 Gutenberg began printing on a wooden **printing press** with a movable bed, which was capable of running 50 sheets an hour. According to one historian, the first cylinder press was invented in 1790, by William Nicholson, of England. It was made of wood and had leather inking rollers. This is regarded as the forerunner of the modern cylinder press.

Halftones came into use about 1885, and in order to print them successfully, more rigid impressions, more thorough ink distribution, harder packing, and dry, smooth-surfaced paper were required. From this time on, better and faster printing presses and superior materials were produced, until today the printing press is a precision machine.

The pressman may take an impression of a form containing gradations in density varying from possibly a square foot or more of solid color to the most delicate vignettes. Perhaps part of the form is of rigid type metal, and part halftones or etchings mounted on wood blocks which will yield under the pressure necessary to print. It naturally follows that, because of unequal contact between the printing surfaces and the paper, some parts of such a form will show a weak print. Under such circumstances, the pressure exerted by a patch of tissue paper 0.001 inch thick might be sufficient to lift the job of printing from mediocrity into art, and lengthen the life of the form.

In printing, it is the appearance of the printed sheet that counts, and with the pressman rests the final outcome. Ignorance, carelessness, or extravagance in the pressroom may waste the finest materials; while on the other hand, the carefully trained pressman assembles his materials so as to produce creditable work. To accomplish this, he is limited only by the quality of the materials with which he works.

QUESTIONS FOR STUDY AND DISCUSSION

1. What conditions in presswork make it necessary to have flexible rules and procedures?
2. To what kind of work is the apprentice pressman often assigned?
3. What essential quality should be practiced from the beginning?
4. Where is printing said to have originated?
5. Name several products essential to presswork.
6. Where was paper first made?
7. By what means was ink formerly distributed over the form?
8. Why is it necessary for rollers to be made accurately?
9. Of what may forms be composed?
10. What influence did the introduction of halftones have on printing?

CHAPTER 3

Printing Processes and Printing Media

SUBJECT OUTLINE

A. Letterpress process:
 1. Movable type.
 2. First power cylinder press.
 3. Linotype.
 4. Monotype.
 5. Halftone screen.
B. Planographic process:
 1. Lithography.
 2. Limestone plates.
 3. Color lithography.

 4. Zinc and aluminum plates.
 5. Offset printing:
  a. Photographic process.
  b. Two-color presses.
  c. Four-color presses.
C. Intaglio process:
 1. Gravure.
 2. Rotogravure.
 3. Embossing.
 4. Thermography.

In this chapter, the three principal printing processes, letterpress or relief, planographic, and intaglio, will be discussed. Of these, the **letterpress process** is the one in which we are most concerned. Relief printing, which is printing from raised characters, is the oldest of the three methods now in use, dating back to the stone carvings of prehistoric man, which have left a continuous pattern through centuries of the graphic arts. Down through the ages man has laboriously tried to write and print, using various media such as crude stone letters, wood carvings, ivory blocks, etc.

Printing from **movable type** was practiced in Europe by Johann Gutenberg in the 15th century. This method of printing gave great impetus to the art, and soon thereafter printing establishments began to spring up in all parts of continental Europe. Between the years A.D. 1500 and 1800 there was comparatively little change in the basic principles of printing presses, but early in the 19th century, the **first power cylinder press** was built in London. This kind of press appeared shortly thereafter in America.

Previous to the year 1886, all relief types were either cast by hand or stamped by the use of dies. About that time, Mergenthaler produced the linotype, and Lanston followed shortly thereafter with the monotype casting machine. The halftone screen also was introduced, which provided for the reproduction of illustrations by photomechanical processes.

The second method of printing to be discussed is the planographic. In this process, printing is done from a flat surface plate which is chemically treated to attract and to hold moisture over the nonprinting areas, and to attract and hold the greasy ink over the printing areas when the plate is dampened. Water and grease naturally will not mix. The image on the plate repels water and attracts ink. The printing machines used for this process are somewhat similar in appearance to the printing presses used in the relief process. However, they are equipped with two sets of rollers, one to distribute the moisture or water, and the other to distribute the greasy ink.

About the year 1800, Alois Senefelder of Bavaria introduced the lithographic process. The word "lithography" is derived from the Greek words "lithos" a stone, and "graphos" to write. Senefelder's first ambition was to study law, but he later turned to playwriting and acting. Although one of his early plays was quite successful, it required all his profits to have it printed, so he decided to produce a cheaper method of printing. His experiments were not entirely successful, but he did devise an important means of duplicating pictures, paintings, drawings, and anything which could be written or photographed.

In Senefelder's early experiments, his attempts to etch copper proved too costly, so he used tiles made of limestone from his district. These were less expensive and produced the same results. His first success was accidental. He had written on one of the stones with some hardened ink he was using at the time, and after it had stood for several days the stone and ink produced the results for which he had been striving. Many improvements on his discovery brought about the satisfactory method of lithography in use today. Senefelder trained many successful lithographers whose works of art are still prized.

The kind of stone used in the lithographic process to hold the form or printing surface was found in various parts of the world, including the United States. However, the best stone for this purpose came from Bavaria and was the same kind as that used by Senefelder. The stones used were from 3 to 4 inches thick, the edges generally were rounded, and the surface cleaned and polished. The surface would have been grained when a stippled or crayon effect was desired. The design to be printed was then drawn directly on the stone, or it may have been drawn on paper and transferred to the stone by pressure and dampening.

Lithography was first used in America in 1819 by Bass Otis, a painter, who drew on stone obtained from Bavaria. The new process was quickly accepted in this country by many famous artists of the period. Lithographs printed in black, and later, hand-colored, were the principal illustrations used in books printed at that time. Many lithograph printing plants were established to meet the demand for their production.

There is some difference of opinion as to when color lithography was first used in this country, but it was probably between the years 1845 and 1850. Crude printing machines, unsatisfactory colored inks, and the poor register of the sheets being printed constituted early drawbacks. In the last half of the 19th century, color lithography advanced rapidly. Most of the color printing, such as Christmas cards, greeting cards, weekly magazines, posters, illustrations, etc., was done by this process.

Lithography was the king of color printing until about 1900, when the letterpress industry started to use the process method of color printing, in which only the three primary colors, red, blue, and yellow, are used. Process or three-color printing is not possible in the stone lithographic method. In order to produce lithograph color work the colors must be applied one at a time. On many of the finer works, 10 separate impressions must be made, or 1 impression for each color or shade of color used.

Zinc and aluminum plates were sometimes used as substitutes for limestone on flatbed presses, but they are most often used in printing on direct rotary lithograph presses. When zinc and aluminum plates were used, rubber rollers were substituted for the calfskin rollers of the flat-stone process.

The lithograph method of printing was the forerunner of the modern **offset printing** process. Offset printing is a **photographic process**, in which the design is photographed onto a positive plate. Many different types of work can be produced by the offset method, such as letterheads, catalogs, books, letters, publications, line drawings, illustrations, and halftone reproductions. Halftone reproductions can be made on rough paper, which is practically impossible in ordinary letterpress printing.

The modern offset press has three cylinders, one above the other: the top cylinder, which contains the printing plate; the middle cylinder, which contains a rubber blanket to be printed by the plate cylinder; and the lower cylinder, which carries the paper to be printed. The ink on the blanket is offset to the paper which travels between the transfer cylinder and the impression cylinder.

Shortly after 1900, several manufacturers began experiments with the offset process. Among them were the Harris Brothers and Ira W. Rubel. Rubel later changed his name twice, his final name being Potter. He was a lithographer, and it was his plan to sell his new machine to only a few of the leading lithographers in this country. In the meantime, however, the Harris Brothers had been successful with their experiments, so machines were soon made available by both companies to anyone who wished to buy.

The work produced by the early offset presses could not compare with that of the old lithograph process. The outstanding advantage was speed, as the older lithograph presses made before 1875 averaged less than 50 impressions an hour, whereas the new power-driven machines in some cases averaged nearly 1,000 impressions per hour. Constant improvements and the entry of new manufacturers in the field have produced outstanding results.

Two-color machines soon came into use and were followed about the year 1931 by **four-color** offset presses. The output of these 4-color presses is equal to 14,000 single color copies an hour. Although process printing was used first on letterpress, it is now often done on multicolor offset presses. Roll-fed offset presses are now being used, as well as sheet-fed machines.

The third principal printing process listed at the beginning of the chapter is **intaglio** or the cutting-in or engraving method of printing. This includes gravure and embossing.

Gravure is the most common application of intaglio printing. The original gravure method was developed from the methods used in printing textiles. The first gravure press was built in England in the latter part of the 18th century. In that press, the design to be printed was engraved intaglio, that is, the design was below the surface on a copper cylinder. With the discovery of light-sensitive materials and of the halftone screen during the latter part of the 19th century, great improvement was made in the gravure processes. At the turn of the 20th century, rotogravure printing obtained real prominence, and the rotogravure picture section of the Sunday newspapers became commonplace.

The gravure plate, which is usually made photomechanically, consists of a series of minute wells of varying depths, which give the gradation in ink tone values. The ink is transferred from these minute wells to the paper by means of impressing the paper into the intaglio wells. For **rotogravure printing**, the form on the press consists of a steel cylinder with a coating of copper which is about $\frac{3}{16}$ of an inch thick. Designs are etched with acid into the copper surface from positive photographic films. The blank parts of the plate then become the surface of the cylinder. This cylinder or form revolves through a trough of ink, and emerges dripping with ink. A thin steel blade, called "the doctor," runs the length of the form, oscillating across the form and removing all excess ink. The only ink then remaining in the form is in the recessed wells.

The paper to be printed then passes between the copper form cylinder and impression cylinder. The depth of the wells determines the amount of ink which is transferred to the surface of the paper. Before being perfected or backed up, the printed sheet is first partially dried by being passed through a heated box or around a steam cylinder. After it is printed on the reverse side it is again dried, and then may be folded and delivered. Despite the difficulty in drying the ink in the rotogravure process, modern newspaper presses are capable of turning out 60,000 four-page supplements an hour.

Embossing is used to improve the appearance of various kinds of printed matter. It may be done on the ordinary style letterpress or cylinder press; but for careful work such as letterheads, specially built embossing presses are used. These presses sometimes have a specially heated bed to insure better embossing. Good results may also be obtained from a heavily built platen press, provided the form to be printed is not too heavy.

A new process, **thermography**, has now almost replaced the old style of embossing. In this process, the work is first printed on the platen or letterpress, and as the printed sheets are delivered from the press they are dusted with a specially prepared powder which clings to the wet ink. Any surplus of powder remaining on the sheet is removed and the sheet is passed under heat which fuses the powder. This application of heat causes the printed areas on the sheet to rise, giving much the same appearance as embossing or skillful engraving. This method may also be used with several different colors, which is a difficult procedure in embossing. Machines now in use will receive the sheets on delivery from the press, automatically remove the excess powder, apply the heat, and deliver the finished product. The process of thermography has greatly improved the appearance of ordinary letterpress production.

In this chapter the three principal methods of printing have been brought to your attention. Most of our work will be with the letterpress method, but later you will become somewhat acquainted with the modern lithograph or offset style of printing also.

QUESTIONS FOR STUDY AND DISCUSSION

1. Name the three principal printing processes in use today.

2. Who is credited with being the first in Europe to use movable type?

3. When was the first power cylinder press built?

4. Which one of the three principal printing processes is in most common use at the present time?

5. What is the fundamental principle of the planographic printing process?

6. Who introduced the lithographic process?

7. Who was the first in the United States to use the lithographic process?

8. When was color lithography first used in the United States?

9. What kind of plates are used in lithographic printing?

10. What process is used in offset printing?

11. Who were prominent in the development of offset printing?

12. What progress has been made in the art of color printing by the offset process?

13. In what way does intaglio printing differ from letterpress or planographic?

14. What is meant by "rotogravure"?

15. When is embossing used?

16. Describe the process known as "thermography."

CHAPTER 4

Press Controls and Safety

SUBJECT OUTLINE

A. Three safety factors.
B. Early printing presses.
C. Later improvements.
D. Belt-driven power machinery.
E. Direct-drive electric-power machinery.
F. Two general groups of machines.
G. Control of speed.
H. Power controls:
   1. Master switch.
   2. Press breaker box and rheostat.
   3. Press control box mounted on the press:
     a. Lever-action switch.
     b. Two-button switch.
     c. Other control boxes.
   4. Belt-tightening device.
   5. Web-press control.
I. Mechanical controls:
   1. Control impressions.
   2. Regulate brakes.
J. When and how to start presses.
K. Stopping the press.
L. Mechanical trip devices.
M. Caution in operating electrical switches.

Anyone who works around machinery should be master of the machine with which he works and should have thorough knowledge of its controls and adjustments so that its operation is second nature to him. Difficult adjustments and problems will be considered later.

Three safety factors should be considered at all times: safety for the operator, safety for others, and safety for the machine and equipment. Carelessness in the pressroom cannot be tolerated.

The **early printing presses** used by Gutenberg and his associates were operated by the strong arm of the pressman. They were made of wood, and the only operation necessary was to bring the platen down to the surface of the form. The platen was lowered by means of a screw located in a cross member, a projecting lever operating the screw. By pulling on this lever, the platen was lowered to the form. A reversal of this procedure raised the platen from the form, and the printing of the sheet was completed.

Later improvements included a sliding bed operated by hand power, and machines which were operated by hand power supplied by a crank which was turned by an assistant. Eventually, presses similar to the platen in present use appeared. These were operated by a foot pedal which was worked simultaneously with the feeding of the press.

Then **belt-driven power machinery** appeared, the power being obtained from a centrally located engine and transferred to the various presses by means of shafts, pulleys, and leather or canvas belts. The engine was driven by steam or gasoline, and in some cases, by water. The disadvantages of belt-driven machinery may readily be seen. The power from the central engine had to be maintained continuously, regardless of the number of presses in operation. The extreme length of the shafts and belts caused much loss of power from friction. The overhead belts and shafts contributed to poor working and lighting conditions. Presses were necessarily arranged in orderly rows, without much regard to light from windows. The overhead arrangement also caused dirt, oil, and dust to be thrown over the machines and piles of paper.

The **direct-drive electric-power unit** in use today superseded the centrally located engine. The advantages of an individual electric motor over the old belt-driven design may be seen readily. Available space may be used to better advantage with regard to light and general working conditions. The number of breakdowns or shutdowns due to failure of the centrally located engine are also greatly reduced. Each press may be run at any desired number of revolutions per hour. This was impossible with the belt-driven machinery, as only two or three variable-speed pulleys were used. The quality of work is improved by greater cleanliness in workrooms. Makeready time is shortened because direct-drive presses can be stopped or started easily. Printing plants may now be located centrally in the business district. This was not always possible when centrally located engines were used as the source of power, due to city ordinances. Probably the most important advantage is the safety features which have been incorporated.

Two general groups of machines used in the printing trade are driven by electric power. The first group includes those machines operated at constant speed, such as paper cutters, stitchers, and other machines used in bookbinding; machines used in electrotyping and stereotyping; and composing-room machinery. The second group, and that which most directly concerns the pressman, includes machines operated at controlled speeds. Almost all power-driven presses are in this group.

Speed is very important and must be regulated to meet the particular needs of the individual job; the limitations of the press, which may vary with the size of sheet being printed; and the individual needs of the human press feeders, which will vary with their abilities. Correct press speed affords great savings by insuring the economical use of stock, press time, and equipment. Both stock and equipment could be seriously damaged if the press were run at too great speed and provisions were not made for stopping it promptly.

Let us first consider the nature and location of the electrical **power controls**. All press groups or individual presses are operated by a series of electrical switches. The first of these is the **master switch**, which is generally located some distance from the individual machine and is not usually the concern of the pressman running the press.

The next switches to be considered are the individual **press breaker boxes and rheostats**. These may be mounted either on the wall convenient to the press or on the press itself. The breaker lever should be thrown to the off position at the close of the work period and when the pressman leaves the machine for any length of time.

Individual **press control boxes** are so **mounted on the press** as to be convenient for all running, makeready, and adjustment operations. These switches are of many styles, varying with the machines on which they are used. One of the oldest still in use is the **lever-action switch**. This consists merely of a single control unit, which is operated by a small arm or lever. Two small hinges keep the lever in the center neutral position. The top hinge is disengaged and the lever raised to its uppermost position to run the press forward. When the lever is placed in its lower position, the press will reverse. The hinges are so constructed and beveled that it is necessary only to lower or raise the lever to the neutral point to return it to the off or stop position.

Another kind of simple control is the **two-button switch** which is used on presses requiring a forward motion only. One button starts the individual press motor and the other stops it. **Other control boxes** have three, four, five, or more buttons, depending on the press requirements. The three-button type has a starting button, a stopping button, and a reverse button. The four-button switch has also a button for inching the press. Pressure on this button will cause the press to move forward; when pressure is released, the press will stop.

The vertical presses in the Letterpress Division are equipped with a two-button control of a different type. The motor which drives the press runs at a constant speed. While it is running and the pumps are in working order, the press can remain stationary. This press is equipped with what is known as a **belt-tightening device**. A pull on the lever which is mounted on the left side of the machine, toward the feeder, tightens the belt on an idling pulley, and the press is put into motion forward. No reverse is possible. The speed is regulated by the size of the drive pulley used. Pulleys may be quickly interchanged by swinging up the belt guard, changing the pulley, and replacing the guard. This belt-tightening drive has advantages over direct drive which will be discussed later.

Most of the presses in the Office are equipped with controls similar to those described. In the operation of **web-fed rotary presses**, however, other **controls** are needed and used. Web presses, because of their size and nature, must have controls located at various points of vantage. These individual controls usually vary in number from 3 to 10 for each press. On the rotary web-fed presses no reversing buttons are used. The most simple control is of the lever type, similar to the one previously described, except that just below the lever two buttons are mounted, one marked "fast" and the other "slow." After the press has been started with the lever, it is speeded up by depressing the fast button until the required press speed is obtained. When the slow button is depressed, the machine speed gradually decreases. There are only two presses which have this type of installation.

The smaller webs are equipped with several single-button stations which serve as safety devices and also as direct-control points. Mounted directly above the single button is a small lever which may be placed in the "safe-and-inch," or "run" position. When the lever is on "safe and inch," the press cannot be started from any control station except the one where the lever is positioned.

The larger web presses are equipped with warning systems on the control boxes, and signals must be transmitted before the press will move. These signals may consist of the ringing of a bell, the flashing of the press lights, or a combination of both.

In the interest of safety and ease of operation, new improvements are constantly being made. One important thing to remember about almost every control, however, is that the "stop" button will protrude from ½ to 1 inch beyond the other control buttons. This is a safety precaution. A general slap at the control box will stop the machine.

In addition to the power controls, all presses are equipped with several **mechanical controls**. These usually **control** the **impression** and **regulate** the press **brake**. On the platen presses, the impression is applied by a hand lever. This lever is pulled toward the feeder to put the press on impression, and the sheet is printed between the platen and the form. When this lever is pushed away from the feeder, the press is placed in the "off" position, so that it will not print.

On some flat-bed presses, the impression is controlled by the foot trip, which is located on the platform at the control side of the press to the right or nearest the feeder. When this pedal is depressed, or depressed and locked, the impression is off. To lock the pedal, it is pushed down and the foot moved to the left. To unlock it, the foot is moved slightly to the right, allowing the pedal to rise and the press to print. On small automatic presses, the impression device is regulated by an automatic mechanical suction trip. All presses are equipped with mechanical brakes or, as is the case with some of the larger web presses, power brakes operating directly on the driving motor. The foot brakes on the platen presses are located directly beneath the flywheel.

On the flatbed Miehle, the brake pedal is similar to the trip pedal, but is mounted forward of the trip, and is operated in the same manner. On the vertical press, the brake is operated by the same lever which tightens the belt. When this lever is thrown to the left or toward the forward part of the press, the brake is applied. No special controls other than the stop button are used to operate those presses equipped with a power brake. When the stop button is depressed, the power brake is automatically applied.

Let us consider **when presses should be started and how to start them.** Before any machine is started, a thorough inspection should be made so that damage to the machine or any of its parts may be avoided. In starting the platen press, be sure this preliminary examination is made. Then depress the run button with the right hand and at the same time give the flywheel a start forward with the left hand. To start the vertical press, first make the preliminary examination of the machine, then turn on the electric motor and pull the belt-tightening lever slowly to the rear. Do not snap this lever back sharply, as damage may result to the press and belt.

On the larger machines, such as the cylinder press, examine the machine and then make sure that no other person is working at any point around the press before starting it. It is best to start the machine at slow speed, either by using the "inch" button or the "slow speed" running button. A good practice to follow when starting the cylinder press is to have one finger on the run button and the other just above the stop button, in case an emergency should develop. When any controls with the signal warning device are used, such as those on web presses, ample time should be allowed for the warning device to operate before the run button is pushed. Whenever an operator is working away from the master control on the web press, a press safety should be used so that the machine cannot be moved.

The brake should not be applied to stop the press while the power is still on, but the stop button should be pushed first and then the brake applied. With a little practice the press may be stopped readily at any desired position. On the belt-tightening and power-brake presses, the power is automatically shut off before the brake is applied. On the vertical press never push the stop button until the brake has been applied.

Care must be exercised at all times when **mechanical trip devices are used**. The hand levers should not be pulled sharply or slammed from one position to another. The same principle applies to the use of the foot trip. Unnecessary roughness in the use of the trip devices may result in serious mechanical troubles. An important point to remember at this time is that, when the Miehle flatbed or any press with a similar trip is running, the pressman should not stand on the control platform with any part of the foot under the trip. If the press should throw off automatically, the trip will be sharply depressed and may cause injury.

The exercise of **caution when operating electrical switches** cannot be too strongly urged. Power controls should not be operated while the hands are wet, or while any rags containing combustible fluids such as gasoline or kerosene are carried in the hand which operates the switch. Keep all electrical switches around the machine free from oil at all times. Turn off all electrical switches at the close of each work period.

Remember that all safety devices, whether mechanical or electrical, are to be used at all times. Anyone who works on any large press where such devices are not available should keep the pressman informed as to his whereabouts at all times.

QUESTIONS FOR STUDY AND DISCUSSION

1. What three safety factors should be considered at all times?
2. How were the early printing presses operated?
3. Discuss some of the disadvantages of the old belt-driven power machinery.
4. What are some of the advantages of the direct-drive electric-power unit now in general use?
5. What two general groups of machines in the printing trade are driven by electric power?
6. Why is it important to be able to control the speed at which a machine operates?
7. Where is the master switch generally located?
8. Where are the individual press breaker boxes and rheostats located?
9. Describe the operation of the belt-tightening device used on the vertical press.
10. What other controls are needed on the web-fed rotary presses?
11. By what means are the impression and brake controlled?

12. What precautionary measure should be taken before starting a press?

13. What precautions are necessary in stopping a machine?

14. What care should be exercised when mechanical trip devices are being used?

15. What special precautions are needed when operating all electrical switches?

CHAPTER 5

Letterpress Printing Machines

SUBJECT OUTLINE

A. Inking unit:
1. Pyramid.
2. Ink plate.
B. Printing unit:
1. Three methods of obtaining an impression:
a. Platen—two flat surfaces.
b. Flatbed—a flat and a curved surface.
c. Rotary—two curved surfaces:
(1) Direct.
(2) Indirect.

2. The cylinder adjustment:
a. Correct surface travel or pitch line.
b. Pressure.
c. Compression.
C. Feeding unit:
1. Sheet separation.
2. Forwarding the sheet.
3. Registering the sheet.
D. Delivery unit.

The operation of press controls and safety precautions which should be observed when working with printing machines have been discussed, and now the fundamentals of letterpress printing machines will be considered. All presses used in printing must have four principal mechanisms or units: one to supply ink to the form, another to provide the impression or transfer of ink from the form to the paper, another to feed the paper to the printing parts, and still another to deliver the sheets after they are printed. From the earliest press to the most modern, all must have these four units, regardless of whether they are hand or mechanically operated.

All **inking units** are similar. They consist of an ink reservoir or fountain, a series of rollers to distribute the ink, and rollers to transfer the ink to the form. The shorter presses generally use a **pyramid** style of roller arrangement with no ink plate or a very small one. The longer presses use an **ink plate** to transfer the ink from the distributor rollers to the form rollers. Presses with ink plates generally use more form rollers than do presses with the pyramid style of inking, to distribute the ink satisfactorily to the form. The means employed to set the rollers vary with the make of the press.

In all relief printing the **printing unit** obtains an impression by one of **three methods**: two flat surfaces may be brought together to produce an impression, or a flat and a curved surface, or two circular surfaces. The oldest, the **platen unit**, holds the form on a flat surface and the sheet to be printed is brought against the form by a flat surface. Platen machines may be sheet-fed or, as on a few presses, roll-fed. Some of the more elaborate presses have a number of platen printing units arranged in a series which produce work in several colors and are fed from rolls of paper.

Several different methods are used to bring the **two flat surfaces** together for parallel impression. For various jobs requiring different packing thickness, either the platen or bed of this kind of press is adjustable to obtain parallel contact. Because of the tremendous pressure required to print from two flat surfaces, platen presses are rigidly constructed. The additional weight of such construction slows their operating speed as compared with other kinds of small presses.

A **flatbed** printing unit is one which has a **flat form** and the sheet or web to be printed on a **curved surface** as the impression is delivered. The majority of machines used in letterpress printing are flatbed. There are many varieties of these presses, but on most of them the cylinder is raised and lowered in fixed bearings as the form or bed moves back and forth under it. This may provide one impression to only one side of the sheet, or, by the addition of another bed and impression cylinder, both sides or the same side in two colors may be printed.

In another kind of flatbed press, the bed remains stationary and the cylinder moves and revolves back and forth over the bed. This arrangement is generally used on proof presses, although some web-fed presses print both sides of the sheet by using two cylinders and two beds, the cylinders revolving in each direction as the sheet is printed. On still another kind of flatbed press, the vertical, the form and the cylinder move in opposite directions during printing.

Rotary presses are those printing machines on which the impression is made between **two curved surfaces**. These presses may be either sheet-fed or web-fed, and with few exceptions the form consists of plates which are curved to conform to the surface of the plate cylinder. Rotary presses may be designed to print only one impression on one side of the sheet, or to print both sides, or to print in colors on one or both sides.

The **rotary presses** used for letterpress printing are **direct rotary** machines, which means that the print is made directly from the form to the paper. Other printing processes which employ direct rotary printing units are gravure, aniline, and several newer methods.

Indirect rotary presses use three cylinders instead of two to obtain an image on the sheet. The inked portion of the plate cylinder is transferred to an intermediate cylinder, from which the ink is placed on the paper held on the impression cylinder. Offset presses are indirect rotaries which are designed with the same capabilities as the direct rotary sheet-fed and web-fed presses.

The necessity for the accurate setting of the flat surfaces on platen presses has already been discussed. When one or more cylinders are part of the printing unit, accurate **cylinder adjustment** is essential, as it is necessary that the two surfaces, the form and the sheet to be printed, travel at as nearly the same speed as possible. This equal speed is known **as correct surface travel** and must be considered at all times. In pressroom terminology, correct surface travel is more commonly known as the **pitch line**. The pitch line refers to an imaginary line on which two contacting gears travel at exactly the same speed. As both the impression cylinder and the part of the printing unit which carries the form are gear driven, it is of utmost importance that these parts travel at the same speed as their driving gears.

A great many factors influence surface travel, among them being form and packing heights, cylinder settings, press construction and erection, and form compressibility. This subject requires lengthy discussion and will be dealt with more fully later.

Equal form and cylinder speeds may not seem too important to the inexperienced, but the experienced pressman knows that incorrect and unequal travel results in poor register on the printed sheet, as the print may be longer or shorter than the form from front to back; unsatisfactory printing, such as slurs or wrinkles; excessive form wear, which produces poor printing on long runs; torn packings, which may result in serious form or press damage; or unusual mechanical strains which shorten the life of the printing machine.

The two printing parts of most flatbed presses and many rotary machines are equipped with bearers, which are metal strips or collars approximately the same height as the printing surface of the form and also of the sheet to be printed as it is held on the impression cylinder. Presses are manufactured so that if the two parts of the printing unit are set to contact each other properly during the printing revolution, that is, with the bearers of an empty press together, the surface travel of the bearers will be the same speed as the pitch line of the gears. Both flatbed and rotary presses have settings which insure that the bearers will remain in contact even while heavy forms are being printed.

Some rotary presses do not use bearers, but settings are provided to keep the two parts of the printing unit in firm contact. It is also important that the cylinders of rotary presses be parallel to maintain correct surface travel, and there are mechanical settings to insure this.

It might seem at first glance as though the two parts of the printing unit must of necessity travel at the same speed as the gears, but unfortunately for the press operator, this is not so. If the circumference of the printing part differs from that of the pitch line of the gear which drives it, correct surface travel will be impossible. In letterpress printing, the sheet to be printed and the form from which it is printed must be brought together under **pressure** in order to transfer the ink to the paper. To produce accurate pressure, the height of the form or the height of the impression cylinder must be adjusted. As various forms require different amounts of pressure, it may be assumed that accurate surface travel in letterpress printing is never attained, but it is the responsibility of the pressman to approach as nearly as possible correct travel between these two printing parts.

The pressure required to print on flatbed or rotary presses is considerably less than that on platen presses. Even though much larger forms are printed on these machines, only a small portion of the form is printed at one time because one or both parts of the printing unit are circular. On flatbed presses enough pressure is required to print at one time a line one-quarter of an inch wide and as long as the form from bearer to bearer. On rotary presses, less pressure is required for a form of equal size because the two contacting printing parts are curved.

It should be remembered that on any press more pressure is necessary to print a solid than a small form area, and the pressure required must be regulated by the pressman by increasing either form or cylinder heights or both.

Most presses are so solidly constructed that the effects of the pressure necessary to print on the machine can hardly be detected. However, on some solid forms the effort to force the printing units apart is noticeable and must be compensated for by the pressman.

As pressure is provided, **compression** enters the picture. This term refers to the give of various factors under stress which may affect the packing, the form, or the paper being printed. It is the responsibility of the pressman to overcome any such compression.

As the impression cylinder of the printing unit must carry a packing of from 0.050 to 0.105 inch thick, depending on the press, the compression of this soft covering during the impression is very great. The degree of compression of the packing may be controlled by the kind and arrangement of the paper or other material used for the packing. The use of various kinds of packing is very important in presswork and will be explained later.

The materials used to make up the form from which the impression is obtained are many and the degree of compression is an extremely variable factor. If plates are mounted on wood blocks, these blocks may compress a great deal under pressure. Metal bases, type, and various kinds of plates are affected differently by pressure, and the impression must be regulated to compensate for this.

Paper on which the job is being printed is very compressible, soft thick paper being affected more than hard-surfaced stocks. Fortunately for the pressman, this factor is easily corrected. Because the regulation for compression requires pressure or height adjustments in either the form or the packing, surface travel may be disturbed unless the pressure needed for printing is distributed carefully.

It was necessary that the early printing machines be fed by hand, but about the year 1900, the first successful automatic feeding machines made their appearance. **Hand feeding** was a costly operation because of slower press speeds, more frequent stops to replenish the supply of stock, and greater sheet spoilage. **Automatic feeders** did not immediately eliminate all these troubles, but steady improvements have been made.

Web-fed presses are fed from rolls of paper, and the feeding has always been mechanical. Improvements on these machines have eliminated the necessity for stops to change rolls. The press continues to run while the new roll is spliced automatically to the old roll.

In order to deliver a single sheet to the press, the **feeder unit**, human or mechanical, must perform three distinct operations. One sheet must first be separated from the others in the pile; it must then be forwarded to the printing unit of the machine; and finally, just before it is printed, two of its edges must be positioned to guides to insure that all sheets have the same register.

While the sheet-feeding mechanism at first glance seems very complicated, it should be realized that all parts are synchronized to run in unison. Once the pressman has mastered the operation of one of the large feeders, he should have little trouble with others. All feeders must complete the three operations previously described and, while the adjustments and settings may vary somewhat, the principle is the same.

Sheet separation may be accomplished in any one of three ways, or sometimes by a combination of the three: corner separation, combing separation, or blast and suction separation.

In corner separation, one or both back corners of the top sheet are detached from the rest of the pile and lifted by suction, and the sheet is completely separated by air blast. This is the method used on most of the large pile feeders.

In combing separation the stock is rolled out in a bank about 2 inches thick, and the sheets are separated by rotary combers which ride on the top of the bank. Friction causes the top sheet to separate from the remainder of the stock and it is forwarded by wheels which drop on its front edge. This principle is generally used on continuous feeders.

Small presses have feeders which separate the sheets by air blast and suction. The top sheet is floated by blast and completely separated by suction feet, wheels, or other devices.

Two methods are in general use to **forward the sheet** to the press guides. The sheet may be carried to the guides by suction or mechanical grippers, as on small presses, or conveyed by tapes or wheels, as on the large machines. The forwarding of the sheets is a simple operation and requires little explanation.

The device used to **register the sheet** to the press side guide may be one of three: The push guide is a block or plate which moves against the guide edge of the sheet and pushes it to register position. The pull guide is a gripper device which moves to the guide edge of the sheet, closes upon it, and pulls the sheet to register against the guide and release it. The rotary guide operates in much the same manner as the pull guide. It has two rollers, one above and one below the sheet, one being friction driven and the other gear driven. The sheet is placed between these open rollers and when they close, the sheet is pulled to side register.

Variations and combinations of these three styles are used on some feeders. Tension on the side-guide mechanism is controllable so that the sheet may be registered sideways gently without jamming, buckling, or bouncing away from the guide.

The **delivery** of the sheets after they are printed is accomplished in either of two ways: The sheet may be removed from the printing surface by suction or mechanical grippers; or the front edge of the sheet may be lifted to strip it from the cylinder, after which it is carried to the jogger or delivery pile by tapes, sticks, or wheels. Joggers are used on all presses to arrange the printed sheets in an orderly pile.

In conclusion, the apprentice should have little difficulty in mastering any press if he realizes that all printing machines are composed of the four principal units discussed in this chapter, each of which is operated in a limited number of ways.

QUESTIONS FOR STUDY AND DISCUSSION

1. Name the four principal mechanisms or units which all printing presses must have to deliver the printed sheets.

2. What are the two kinds of inking units in general use?

3. Name the three methods used to obtain a printed impression.

4. Describe the means by which an impression is obtained on platen presses.

5. What method obtains an impression on flatbed presses?

6. How is a printed impression obtained on rotary presses?

7. Why is accurate cylinder adjustment necessary?

8. What is meant by the expressions "correct surface travel" and "pitch line"?

9. How may pressure be adjusted?

10. Discuss the difference in the pressure requirements of flatbed and rotary presses.

11. By what means may the effect of compression on packing be controlled? On press forms? On the paper to be printed?

12. When did successful automatic feeding units first appear?

13. Name the three operations which a feeding unit must perform.

14. By what process is the sheet to be fed separated from the pile? Forwarded to the press guides? Registered?

15. Discuss the delivery unit by which the printed sheet is carried to the delivery pile.

CHAPTER 6

Press Sections in the
Letterpress Division

SUBJECT OUTLINE

A. Main Press Section:
  1. Illustration Unit.
  2. Emergency Unit.
  3. Job Unit.

  4. Book Unit.
  5. Web Unit.
B. Postal Card Section.

The Letterpress Division has two principal press sections: the Main Press Section and the Postal Card Section.

The Main Press Section of the Letterpress Division is located on the fourth floor and part of the fifth floor of Building No. 3. This section is subdivided into five units: the **Book, Illustration, Job, Web,** and **Emergency** units. These units produce a variety of book and job work and the majority of this work is produced on flatbed cylinder presses.

In the Job Press Unit work is done that is suited to the special and smaller presses in that section, such as envelopes, cards, letterheads, embossing, numbering, tags, posters, etc.

Many kinds of presses are used in the Job Unit. The first to be considered are the embossing and stamping presses which are equipped to handle up to 1,400 sheets an hour. The larger of these prints a maximum-sized sheet of 14 by 17 inches. White House stationery, invitations, and other similar fine work are embossed on these presses. Special envelope presses print envelopes of various sizes up to 14 by 17 inches. These are small rotary presses, and the plates used are curved rubber plates. Their speed range is from 15,000 to 45,000 an hour.

Another group of small presses includes the platens, all of which are automatically fed. These machines will handle general jobwork and will print up to 3,000 an hour. Some of them are equipped to handle two sheets at once.

The Job Press Unit also has a group of smaller sized cylinder automatics. Some of these machines are equipped to work two sheets at a time. The maximum single-sheet size is 13 by 19½ inches, and the maximum speed is 5,000 an hour. Another group of these smaller size cylinder automatics includes some presses which will print all kinds of paper and card stock automatically, with a maximum speed of 4,000 an hour, the largest size sheet being 20 by 25½ inches.

Another function of the Job Unit is the maintenance and preparation of numbering machines for all number printing in the Main Press.

It is sometimes difficult to differentiate distinctly between job and bookwork. Under certain circumstances work may be interchanged if the presses are available. Generally speaking, however, bookwork consists of printing sheets which must be folded into signatures to be made into books in the bindery, or jobs printed on the web presses which are delivered from the press already folded in signature form, or pasted or wire stitched in completed form.

In the Book Unit some of the presses print on all grades of paper and card stock and are fine for close-registered color and halftone work.

Cylinder presses of various sizes are equipped with automatic feeders, including the latest models suitable for high-grade work. Four of the presses are perfecting presses; that is, they print both sides of the sheet in one operation and have two impression cylinders and two form beds.

This unit contains a security area walled off from the balance of the unit. This security area contains presses of various sizes to handle classified work from an identification card to books of several hundred pages.

The Illustration Unit has a row of automatically fed cylinder presses and it is there that the highest class of illustrations in the Office is produced. Most of the color work is also done in this section. One two-color press handles a maximum size sheet of 32 by 45 inches and prints two colors on the same side of a sheet in one operation, the forms being specially made up to fit this machine. In addition to the presses mentioned there are in the Illustration Section two presses in what is known as the cage, where classified work is printed under supervision.

The Emergency Unit does work which requires immediate printing, such as congressional bills and any other rush work with but little preparation before the press run.

The preliminary printing of patents is also done under the supervision of the Emergency Section. The presswork is performed on four hand-fed cylinder presses and they average 25 eight-page forms each per shift.

The Web Unit presses print both job and book work but the majority of the work produced is of the book variety.

The presses in this unit are located on both the fourth and fifth floors in Building No. 3. The Record presses are located on the fifth floor and are the largest printing machines in the Office. These three Cottrell Record presses, purchased in 1952, were built especially for the Congressional Record. Specifications were drawn up, however, to make these presses versatile enough to handle departmental work of sufficient volume to warrant their use. A typical example of this work is the income-tax program with its complex packaging.

Book web presses are on the fourth floor in the same building as the Record presses. The magazine and speech presses, in addition to the two sheet-fed Miehles and one card press, are also located on this floor. The magazine web presses produce a very satisfactory grade of halftone printing and turn out a large volume of work in a day.

Web presses produce signatures of 4, 8, 16, 24, 32, 48, or 64 pages depending on the press group. Printing is done from electrotype, stereotype, or magnesium plates. Various presses are equipped with pasters, perforators, or stitchers, either separately or in combination.

High running speeds and elimination of some bindery operations help this unit keep pace in this modern era of printing.

The Postal Card Section is located on the second floor of the Government Printing Office Warehouse, which is across the street from the main building. In the card section a group of specially made rotary printing presses print United States postal cards and return cards. It is interesting to note that the daily output of the postal-card presses in this section is around ten million printed cards.

The balance of the section is made up of three presses. Two of these presses have been equipped with folders to deliver a folded product. One of the presses has been redesigned to print air-mail envelopes. The back of the press has been equipped to gum and dry the web of paper before it is printed.

This section is also air conditioned. Of special interest here is the method of handling the rolls of stock. A railroad siding runs in on the third floor of the warehouse, and the rolls of paper used on the postal-card presses are delivered directly from freight cars on this floor and lowered to the pressroom floor by an automatic elevator called a lowerator. By this means a whole carload lot of 1,000-pound rolls can be delivered in 45 minutes.

QUESTIONS FOR STUDY AND DISCUSSION

1. Name the five units of the Main Press.
2. In general, what class of work is done in the Main Press Section?
3. What kind of presses are used in the Book Section?
4. In what classes of work does the Illustration Section specialize?
5. In the Emergency Section what kind of work is printed?
6. Into what two general groups are the web presses divided?
7. What class of work is printed on the speech press? What are the capabilities of these presses?
8. What is the specialty of the Record presses?

CHAPTER 7

Equipment for Presswork

SUBJECT OUTLINE

A. Pressman's individual equipment:
1. Pencils.
2. Makeready knife.
3. Wrenches.
4. Ball peen hammer.
5. Screwdriver.
6. Pliers.
7. Tweezers.
8. Flexible steel tape.
9. Center punch.
10. Nail set.
11. Folding steel rule.
12. Gages.
13. Keys.
14. Carborundum stone.
15. Magnifying glass.
16. Brushes.
17. Calipers.
18. Micrometers.
19. Toolbox.

B. Office tools and equipment.
C. Maintenance Division.

During his course of training, the apprentice pressman may be called upon to make minor adjustments and repairs, so the proper use of tools is important and should be given careful consideration. This chapter deals with the equipment which should be available to the pressman. Samples of various tools will be shown and their use demonstrated during your on-the-job training.

First to be considered is the **pressman's individual equipment**, which he will need to have accessible at all times in order to produce good printing.

He will need two **pencils**, a No. 1 black pencil which is very soft to mark out the sheets in the various makeready processes and a No. 2 black pencil to record the information needed concerning the presswork for record cards and various forms.

Makeready knives come in many styles and their selection is a matter of individual choice. They are used to cut out small pieces of tissue or folio or other stock during the makeready process. Some pressmen regard the manufactured knives as too heavy and cumbersome, so they make their own from a piece of discarded hacksaw blade mounted in wood. The part of the handle holding the hacksaw blade is wrapped with linen twine and varnished or shellacked. This makeready knife is light, easy to use, inexpensive, and easy to carry.

Makeready knives may have either a straight or rounded cutting edge or two cutting edges.

Wrenches of various kinds are needed. Open-end wrenches are used in the ordinary processes of presswork. They have a different size opening on each end. The apprentice will need five of these wrenches with openings varying in size as follows: $\frac{1}{4}$ by $\frac{5}{16}$ of an inch, $\frac{3}{8}$ by $\frac{7}{16}$ of an inch, $\frac{1}{2}$ by $\frac{9}{16}$ of an inch, $\frac{5}{8}$ by $\frac{3}{4}$ of an inch, $\frac{19}{32}$ by $\frac{11}{16}$ of an inch. They will accommodate most of the adjustments to be made on the various presses, but in some cases other kinds of wrenches are needed.

The cylinder-pin wrench is an 8-inch thin steel rod, the fitted ends of which are suitable for various press operations, such as opening cylinder clamps, adjusting bed clamps, etc. One of these pin wrenches is usually found in a special rack on the side of the press, but it is a valuable piece of equipment to own individually.

The 8-inch adjustable crescent wrench is a very handy tool with which to make the many size adjustments necessary around printing presses.

Most of the later presses are equipped with headless recessed screws. The set screw has a hexagonal socket, and the wrench to be used is an L-shaped hexagonal bar made to fit the socket. The screws and wrenches vary in size. A complete set of the necessary wrenches will prove a valuable and inexpensive addition to the tool kit.

The **ball peen hammer** is a light steel hammer with which many press adjustments may be made. Some pressmen prefer a bronze-headed hammer which prevents damage to the steel or other metal parts of the press. A hammer must always be used with caution to avoid damage to the machine. Various uses may be found for the 8-inch **screwdriver** when press adjustments are being made. Sometimes a smaller or a larger screwdriver may be needed.

For some work, the adjustable **pliers** commonly furnished in automobile kits may be satisfactory. In addition to these, diagonal pliers or wire cutters may be needed for later phases of presswork.

A small pair of **tweezers** is a necessity in the pressroom to pick up or straighten small pieces of type within the form; but they also have various other uses.

A 6-foot flexible **steel tape** is employed to make various measurements of paper and is a necessary piece of equipment for the pressman. It is made of very lightweight steel contained in a case hardly larger than the old dollar watch.

The **center punch** is used by the pressman when working on plates mounted on wooden blocks. Sometimes these plates must be removed from the blocks and later remounted. When they are remounted, new holes must be punched in the edge of the plates, and the center punch is necessary for this purpose.

A **nail set** is used when the tacks holding the plate to the block are finally driven home and also in various operations which require a smaller size pin wrench, such as in setting rollers, etc.

Unlike the 6-foot flexible tape, the 2-foot **folding steel rule** is usually carried by pressmen. It folds together to a 6-inch length and is a very handy piece of equipment for various short measurements in imposing forms and in general work around the press.

Several **gages** are needed, the first being the type-high gage, with which to measure the height of type, block-mounted plates, and plates mounted on patent bases. It is graduated to indicate when type or plates are of the proper height. The roller gage is used to set the rollers to the bed of the press or to type height on presses which contain no inking plates. In later models both these gages are combined in one tool. The thickness gage has leaves of various thicknesses and its function is to measure clearances in presswork.

Two kinds of **keys** are needed. Quoin keys come in two models, the first being the standard or T-type, and the other, known as the gooseneck style, has a key on the end of a long steel rod. These keys are used while type forms are being imposed and to lock forms and bases on the bed of the press. Plate keys lock plates on patent bases. One or two holders will usually accommodate all these keys. They will be discussed further in a later chapter.

Knives, punches, and other pieces of pressroom equipment are sharpened on a **carborundum stone**. Care should be taken to avoid chipping when any sharpening is being done, and the carborundum stone should be cleaned regularly.

Every good pressman needs a **magnifying glass** to enable him to see and correct defects in plates and to see how the printed work is taking on the paper, etc. Small pocket magnifying glasses are satisfactory for this purpose.

The first of the **brushes** needed to clean forms is the ordinary form brush. This is a hair brush, which fits securely in the palm of the hand, the back of which measures about 2 by 4 inches. The second brush is the halftone plate brush. It is similar in size to the form brush, the difference being that it is made of soft copper wire surrounded on all sides by about ¼ inch of hair. This brush is used on electrotype plates and halftone screens, not on type forms.

Calipers are employed to measure the outside and the inside dimensions of various items connected with presswork. They are a convenient item of pressroom equipment.

There are two styles of **micrometers**, the first being the stock micrometer, which opens to a maximum of about ⅜ of an inch. The other is the machinist's 1-inch micrometer, which opens to a maximum of 1 inch. Both these styles are suitable for use in the pressroom, as in many press operations it is valuable to know to the thousandth of an inch the thickness of the paper or plate. They are very delicate instruments which measure the thickness of the paper or the thickness of various blankets and plates. Not many pressmen own a micrometer, as it is an expensive instrument.

Each pressman should have a sturdily built **toolbox**, small enough for easy handling, yet large enough to accommodate all the tools needed. This usually contains a main sector and a tray for smaller pieces of equipment. The tools should be kept clean and placed in the toolbox in orderly fashion and easily accessible.

Besides the equipment owned by the pressman, the various sections of the **Office** have additional **tools and equipment** that may be required. These include keys for various plate-locking devices, sandpaper, emery cloth, chalk, different-sized pin wrenches, brads, ink knives, and a large clock-faced micrometer.

Major troubles and adjustments are handled by our capable **Maintenance Division**, which includes the Machine Shop, the Electrical Section, the Pipe Shop, and the Carpenter Shop. All these have specially trained mechanics for the various kinds of work to be done in the Office.

QUESTIONS FOR STUDY AND DISCUSSION

1. As part of the pressman's individual equipment, what kind of pencils are useful?

2. Describe a makeready knife. What is its purpose?

3. What different kinds of wrenches are needed?

4. Why is precaution necessary in the use of the ball peen hammer?

5. Which screwdriver is especially useful?

6. What kind of pliers are needed?

7. Why is a pair of tweezers a necessity?

8. What is the purpose of the 6-foot flexible steel tape in a pressman's work?

9. When plates are to be remounted on blocks, what implement is used to punch new holes? To fasten the plates to the blocks?

10. When is a 2-foot folding steel rule especially useful?

11. Discuss the various gages needed.

12. Describe the keys needed to lock forms.

13. On what kind of stone are knives and other equipment sharpened?

14. For what purpose is a magnifying glass used in presswork?

15. Describe the brushes needed in presswork.

16. Why are calipers necessary?

17. Describe the two styles of micrometers which are specially useful in the pressman's work.

18. Name some of the various equipment provided by the Office for presswork.

19. Which division of the Government Printing Office takes care of all machinery adjustments?

CHAPTER 8

Cleaning Pressroom Equipment

SUBJECT OUTLINE

A. Reasons equipment should be kept clean.
B. Cleaning preparations used in the pressroom:
  1. Water and solvents containing water.
  2. Inflammable solvents:
    a. Aviation gasoline.
    b. Oil and kerosene added to motor gasoline.
    c. Pure water-white benzol.
    d. Ink solvent—50 percent benzol and 50 percent acetone.
    e. Kerosene.
  3. Noninflammable solvents:
    a. Carbon tetrachloride.
    b. Trisodium phosphate.
C. Methods of cleaning equipment:
  1. Press forms.
  2. Rollers.
  3. Natural-finish press parts.
  4. Zinc press pans.
  5. Cabinets and other painted furniture.
  6. Patent bases.
D. Safety precautions.

Cleaning pressroom equipment is the subject in this lesson. If we expect to be comfortable in the pressroom surroundings and produce good printing, we must keep ourselves and the equipment clean.

The reasons equipment should be kept clean will be discussed first. Clean presses mean better working conditions and result in better printing. If the forms are kept free from dried ink, the sheets printed from them will be more acceptable. Clean forms are more convenient to handle in the pressroom and the composing room. Rollers which are properly cared for distribute the ink more effectively and last much longer than rollers not given adequate care. They should be cared for during the press run as well as when they are stored.

Next to be discussed are the various **cleaning preparations used in the pressroom.** Many of these solvents are toxic to some individuals. Inhalation of the fumes may be harmful or irritation to the skin may result. Necessary precautions must be taken when using solvents which are even mildly toxic. Cleaning solvents should remove all ink, dirt, and oil; should evaporate completely, leaving no film of any kind which might interfere with printing; and should leave the surface of the metal in such condition that it will not be subject to corrosion or rust. As some solvents are inflammable, we should recognize the volatile preparations and observe all precautions.

Water and solvents containing water are used for only a few specific purposes. They do not evaporate quickly enough for the purposes for which they are intended, and they have a tendency to corrode or rust the metal parts of the press. In some cases, such as when watercolor or copying ink are run, water must be used to clean press rollers. When such action is necessary, the rollers should be removed from the machine to be washed, but if this is not possible care should be taken to see that all water is removed from press parts after the washup has been completed. The rollers and parts affected should be given a light film of oil to preserve them.

Inflammable solvents clean ink from type or plates and then evaporate, leaving the surface of the metal free from undesirable oil film.

The one objectionable feature of these volatile solvents is that, while they separate the dried ink from the surface of the form, they allow it to accumulate between the type and in the lower places in the form. This may be partly overcome by a method of cleaning which will be described later.

Most solvents used in the pressroom are inflammable and must be employed with caution. They should be kept away from open flames and never come in direct contact with electrical switches. They should be kept in safety cans with properly fitted covers and stored in places which are as safe as possible, such as metal cabinets.

Many solvents have been used in the past, including aviation gasoline, kerosene, carbon tetrachloride, and trisodium phosphate.

Varsol is now the primary solvent and should be used whenever possible for cleaning needs in the pressroom. The Printing Office uses approximately 900 gallons of this cleaning solvent each week. If ink has dried so hard that the varsol fails to remove it, an ink solvent made in the Government Printing Office should be used. It is made up of 50 percent xylene and 50 percent trichloroethylene. The mixture has a lower toxicity and greatly reduced fire hazard in comparison with many solvents used in the past.

Other more powerful ink solvents are available upon request to remove hardened or dried ink from type or plates when the standard solvents will not work. One in this class is **acetone**, which is distilled from vegetable matter. It has an odor which may be disagreeable to some persons and may also cause headaches and dizziness if inhaled over long periods of time.

Let us now consider the actual **methods of cleaning** the various kinds of equipment. For **press forms**, any of the volatile cleaners necessary may be used. Type forms should be cleaned with the animal-hair brush. The same solvents may be employed on forms containing electrotype or halftone plates, but the wire plate brush should be used. Only a small section of the form should be cleaned at one time. This will prevent the accumulation of ink in the lower portions.

The procedure is as follows: Pour cleaner on the brush, scrub the section of the form to be cleaned, then wipe that section clean, and dry with a clean rag containing no bits of metal or buttons. Avoid inhaling the fumes from the solvents as much as possible. When forms are cleaned on the bed of the cylinder press, it is always best to raise the front hinged section of the feedboard to allow as free circulation of air as possible. Where the feeder is down and the job is being printed, it is not possible to raise the board, therefore extreme caution should be exercised to prevent inhaling the fumes.

A form-washing machine, developed by employees of the Government Printing Office, cleans forms which contain no wooden furniture. This machine, with its endless conveyor chain carrying the chase in vertical position, works automatically. The hot chemical cleansing fluid is sprayed under pressure against both sides of the chase and form. The form then passes through a rinsing spray and drying apron, emerging from the machine thoroughly cleaned and almost dry.

Any of the volatile cleaners already discussed may be employed on any of the various press parts, except ink solvent. Ink solvent is a paint remover and should not be used to clean any of the painted parts. After any press part has been cleaned, it should be rubbed dry with a soft rag.

The **zinc press pans** may be cleaned by any one of several solvents. They are located beneath all pieces of machinery. The most common cleaner is varsol, applied with a mop. The pan is thoroughly cleaned and then mopped dry. Any of the volatile solvents may be used. The pan should be dried with a soft, clean cloth after it has been cleaned.

Patent bases are cleaned by a 2-hour immersion in a tank containing a cleaning solution at the boiling point. They are then rinsed with hot-water spray and dried by compressed air. To prevent rusting, the bases are then treated with a mixture of half lubricating oil and half kerosene. Plate catches used with these bases are cleaned in a similar manner and treated to prevent rusting.

Finally we consider the **safety precautions** which should be observed in all cleaning operations. To avoid personal injury while using any cleaning solvents, avoid inhaling the fumes. To prevent skin irritation, wear rubber gloves when recommended and clean the hands immediately after using solvents. Always shut off the press power when the press is being cleaned, as sparks from faulty electric switches may ignite rags which contain volatile solvents. When cleaning fluids are being used, avoid damage to painted surfaces by employing only those fluids which will not remove the paint or change its color. After any fluids which may cause rust have been used, always apply a light film of oil to the metal. Treat rollers with oil mixed with varsol after cleaning with any solvent which might be harmful to their surfaces. Use rags that are free from buttons or small pieces of metal. Vigorous rubbing with rag or brush may break off pieces of type, so brush type forms gently. Be sure to keep all volatile cleaning fluids and rags used with them in covered containers when they are not in actual use.

QUESTIONS FOR STUDY AND DISCUSSION

1. Why is it necessary to keep all pressroom equipment clean?
2. Name some of the desirable characteristics of an effective cleaning solvent.
3. What undesirable effect does water have on rollers and metal parts of presses?
4. When it is necessary to use water or solvents containing water, what after-care should be given?
5. When inflammable solvents are used, what precautions should be observed?
6. What are the advantages of inflammable solvents? What undesirable feature do they have?
7. When press forms are to be cleaned, what procedure is followed?
8. Describe the form-washing machine used in the Government Printing Office.
9. Which solvent is preferable when rollers are being cleaned?
10. Which solvent may be used effectively to clean natural-finish press parts?
11. How are zinc press pans cleaned?
12. What special cleaning process is applied to patent form bases?
13. Discuss the safety precautions which should be used in all cleaning operations.

CHAPTER 9

The Development of Platen Presses

SUBJECT OUTLINE

A. Platen press defined.
B. The first recorded use of the printing press, Johannes Gutenberg.
C. Notable names in the development of the platen press:
   1. Blaew.
   2. Annison.
   3. Ramage.
   4. Stanhope.
   5. Clymer—Columbian press.
   6. Rust—Washington press.
   7. Adams—the first power platen.
   8. Hawkes.
   9. Ruggles.
   10. Gordon.
   11. Gally—the Universal press.

This is the first of a group of three chapters on the development of printing machines, today's topic being concerned with platen presses. The term "platen press" may be defined as that class of press which has two flat surfaces to be brought into contact to make an impression of the entire surface of the form simultaneously. The platen is that part of the press which gives the impression. In a job press, the platen is that part which carries the packing and the makeready, and upon which sheets are fed to receive the impression.

The principle is similar to that used by the Chinese when they printed upon silk or paper from wooden blocks. They inked the surface of the engraved block and laid the material to be printed on the inked block. Impression, or transfer of ink, was accomplished by the use of hair brushes, which were skillfully manipulated. This was a slow process and required the use of soft ink and very absorbent paper. Furthermore, it was suited only to a country such as China was at that time, where labor was cheap and only a few finished copies were needed. Many examples of this work by the Chinese show that amazing skill was acquired in this process.

Later on in Europe greater speed in printing was required. This brings us to the **first recorded use of the printing press** by **Johannes Gutenberg** about 1450. The extensive use of paper and the invention of ink suitable for mechanical printing contributed to the necessity for a printing press. The first press is thought to be an improvement on the cheese and wine presses in use at the time. Two level surfaces, the bed which held the inked form and the sheet to be printed, and the platen which supplied the impression, were brought together under pressure. The simple form of wooden press used by Gutenberg continued to be used a century and a half without marked changes.

There are many **notable names** connected with the development of the platen press. About the year 1620, **William Jenson Blaew**, of Amsterdam, passed the spindle of the screw through a square block which was guided between upright timbers. From this block the platen was suspended by wires or cords. The block prevented any twist in the platen, gave a more even motion to the screw, and increased the power of the impression. The bed of the Blaew press was stone, the rest wood. After the impression was delivered, the platen raised automatically as the screw was attached to a spring. This improvement practically doubled the speed of earlier presses, since as much time was required to unscrew the platen as to screw it down onto the form.

Blaew also placed a device upon the press to roll the bed in and out, and added a new form of iron lever to turn the screw. The Blaew press was used in England and on the continent extensively. No further improvements in hand presses are recorded until about 1785, when a French printer named **Annison** substituted iron for wooden parts, and incorporated a more powerful lever.

The next great improvement was made by **Adam Ramage**, who, in 1790, began to build presses in Philadelphia. He substituted an iron bed and platen for the wood and stone that had been in use so long and built a much better machine, though still small in size. He used a triple-thread, rapid-motion screw that greatly shortened the lever pull. These presses were much admired, and even as late as 1885 they were still in use as proof presses.

In 1798 the **Earl of Stanhope** in England built a press with a frame of cast iron in one piece, a combination of levers on the screw mechanism allowing a more powerful impression with less labor on the pressman's part. These presses were introduced because wood cuts were coming into use, the tendency was toward larger forms of type, and the necessity had arisen for greater power in giving the impression. The Stanhope press had an iron platen similar to those previously used on wooden presses.

It is interesting to note that up to this time, all platen presses had the same general faults. They were small, the production was slow, and the impression was still being applied by the use of the old hand lever. In 1816, **George Clymer** of Philadelphia produced the first all-iron press, and started a factory in London in 1817. This press was an entirely new departure from the old ideas, and the impression was given by means of a series of compound levers which greatly magnified the power the pressman exerted on the handlebar and eliminated much of the friction of the old screw presses. This press was called the Columbian.

The **Columbian press** was peculiar in appearance because the weight of the platen was counterbalanced by a series of levers terminating in a counterweight in the shape of an eagle. This was the first press built in large sizes which gave a full sheet impression at a single pull of the lever. Earlier presses, because of their limited impression power, were restricted to smaller size sheets. When larger size sheets were required, the impression was applied by two separate operations and forms. Up to this time the maximum platen had been about 12 by 18 inches, but the Columbian had a maximum of 23 by 32 inches.

It is interesting to note that all these early presses used the folding tympan and the folding friskets, and the form and tympan were moved in and out on the bed of the press by hand. In the printing of a single sheet, there were 11 different press operations: The type form was inked by use of the inking balls, the sheet placed on the frisket, the frisket folded on the tympan, the tympan folded on the form, the form rolled in under the platen, the impression applied, the impression released, the form rolled out, the tympan raised, the frisket raised, and the printed sheet removed.

In 1829, **Samuel Rust** perfected the design of a hand press known as the **Washington press**. This press was so far superior to any of the foregoing models that it soon drove its competitors from the market. The lever action was greatly simplified. There were only two working members with a friction roll or pin between them. The power was so magnified that very large sizes were built and operated successfully. Many of these Washington hand presses are still used by photoengravers to pull proofs of their plates. The construction of hand presses which permits an unlimited dwell during the impression makes them ideal for this purpose.

Various means of inking the form on the hand presses had been tried, but until 1830, when composition rollers were invented, no satisfactory method had been discovered. Inking by rubber rollers had been tried. This was only partly successful and was used occasionally on cheap work. The first composition rollers were used singly in a hand frame with two handles; but it was not long before two rollers were used together in the same frame to get better inking and distribution. This was soon followed by a mechanical arrangement of a vibrating cylinder under which two composition rollers were placed. This mechanism was made the full width of the bed, and the form was inked twice for each impression. This greatly increased the output of the hand press and did away with the "roller boy," or the assistant pressman.

Isaac Adams produced the **first power platen press** in Boston in 1830. This press had a stationary platen, but a mechanically driven moving bed. The bed rose for the impression and dropped back again to its lowered position while the inking rollers passed over the form. The inking rollers were drawn in and out by the frame or carriage of the frisket which carried the sheet into printing position. As soon as the advantages of the Adams press were seen, it was constructed with additional rollers, up to as many as six. The Adams press, developed around 1845, did much to revolutionize the printing of illustrated books in America. In the early days of the Government Printing Office, a number of Adams presses were in use. The small presses of this make produced 800 completed copies an hour, while the large presses, 32 by 44 inches, produced 600 per hour. This more than doubled the production of the old hand presses.

A number of inventors entered the platen press field about the year 1850, and laid the foundation for the modern press. In 1850 **Hawkes** designed a press with a fixed form and a traveling roller inker, the platen being oscillated toward and from the form by a crank disk and connecting rod driven from a power belt.

The **Ruggles** press, in 1851, was provided with a fixed form which was the flat side of a cylinder. The remaining surface of the cylinder was used as an ink-distributing surface around which the form rollers traveled. The platen was oscillated toward and from the form by means of a connecting rod and crank disk.

The most important invention of this time was the **Gordon** press, which was first patented in 1851. In it the platen rocked on its center, and the form, after the platen had rocked in vertical position, was driven toward the platen to give the impression by means of a cam and toggle. An ink drum was used at the end of the form to distribute the ink, and the machine was operated by a treadle and flywheel. Gordon presses are still in use today, the modern version having many improvements, including the addition of automatic feeders.

In 1869 **Merritt Gally**, of Rochester, N.Y., made the greatest step forward in platen printing presses that had been made. He invented the **Universal press.** This machine is in a class by itself; and the name Universal has come to be used to designate any press giving perfectly parallel impression in a similar manner. In Gally's machine the platen is a rocker that rolls into feeding position upon flat ways and then rolls back to a perpendicular plane and is pulled directly parallel to the form with a sliding motion. This press has excellent cylindrical ink distribution and is equal to a cylinder press in this respect.

QUESTIONS FOR STUDY AND DISCUSSION

1. How may the term "platen press" be defined?
2. When and by whom was the first recorded printing press used?
3. Describe the press invented by Blaew.
4. What contribution did Annison make toward the development of the platen press?
5. Discuss some distinguishing features of the press developed by Adam Ramage.
6. What factors influenced the necessity for larger presses?
7. What improvement was made by Stanhope?
8. What specially notable feature appeared in Clymer's Columbian press?
9. In what way was Rust's Washington press superior to preceding presses?
10. Who was the inventor of the first power platen? Describe this press.
11. What was a distinguishing feature of the Hawkes press? the Ruggles press?
12. Describe the operation of the Gordon press.
13. Who was the inventor of the Universal press?
14. What general meaning is now given to the term Universal?

CHAPTER 10

The Development of Cylinder Presses

SUBJECT OUTLINE

A. Letterpress machines:
  1. Platen.
  2. Cylinder.
  3. Rotary.
B. Some notable names in the development of cylinder presses:
  1. Nicholson.
  2. Koenig.
  3. Treadwell.
  4. Napier.
  5. Cowper and Applegath.
  6. Hoe.
  7. Dutarte.
  8. Kidder.
  9. Taylor.
  10. Cottrell.
  11. Miehle.

Before considering the development of cylinder presses, let us understand why hand presses, on which all printing was done for nearly 400 years, needed to be improved. In the first place, more speed was needed. The maximum number of impressions a good pressman could produce was approximately 250 an hour. In the second place, the method of applying pressure to the whole form at one time made it impossible for these presses to handle large or solid forms.

Since the 15th century, engravers had been using the kind of press which produced its impression by revolving a wooden roller fixed in stationary bearings over a moving bed. This bed contained the plates, the blanket, and the paper to be printed. The engravers also supplied the idea of using rollers instead of inking balls with which to ink the form.

Let us discuss briefly the **letterpress machines** in use today. First of these is the **platen** press on which the type or form is carried on a flat bed, and the impression is made by the use of a flat platen. Platen presses require a tremendous amount of pressure to print a large form or a form composed of solids. Presses built heavy enough to provide this pressure were expensive, cumbersome, slow, and inadequate.

Koenig also invented a perfecting press; that is, a press having two cylinders and two forms whereon the sheet is printed on both sides in one operation. The use of steam power to drive printing machines was also started in England by Koenig.

In the United States, the first use of steam power to drive printing presses was by **Treadwell** in 1822 in Boston. Treadwell's press was a bed-and-platen machine which was soon outclassed by other presses.

Many improvements were being made on cylinder presses by various inventors and manufacturers, among them **Napier**, who produced continuous-revolution presses about the year 1824. His chief claim to distinction is the invention of grippers. This invention dispensed with the need for friskets or tapes to carry the sheets around the impression cylinder.

Some time between the years 1825 and 1830, Napier introduced in England a press with an impression cylinder of small diameter. In order to allow the form to return under the cylinder after the impression was made, he devised a method of raising and lowering the cylinder and improved the toggle-motion bed mechanism. Napier also introduced a machine that was driven by hand and included a single feedboard and two impression cylinders of small diameter, each with grippers. The sheet was held by a set of grippers, carried around the first impression cylinder and printed on one side, then transferred to a second set of grippers on the other impression cylinder and printed on the reverse side of the paper. The cylinders alternately rose and fell to clear the bed. By that time, press speeds had greatly increased, and as many as 2,000 impressions an hour were produced.

In the year 1827, **William Cowper** and **Ambrose Applegath** invented a four-cylinder press capable of printing between 4,000 and 5,000 sheets an hour. In this machine the bed was vertical, surrounded by four impression cylinders. It had four feedboards. In 1948 the same principle was applied to an eight-impression cylinder press. The bed cylinder was a polygon, and this machine printed 10,000 sheets an hour. These presses were of the rotary type and will be further discussed in the next lesson.

Cowper and Applegath are also credited with several improvements in the cylinder machine about the year 1823. These included a simplified version of Koenig's press and an improved method of placing the distributor inking rollers diagonally on the press table to give the endwise motion of these rollers without additional mechanism. This method is still used.

These deficiencies were overcome by the invention of the cylinder press. This machine carries the form on a flat bed while the impression cylinder moves in geared speed with the form to apply the impression. By this method, a maximum of about ¼ inch impression is applied at a time. Since this impression area stretches across the cylinder, very little pressure is needed, and many of the undesirable features of the platen press have been eliminated.

On the **rotary** press, which uses two cylinders, the impression cylinder is similar to that used on cylinder presses; but the form also is curved around a cylinder, the impression being delivered continuously between the two cylinders.

There are many **notable names** connected with the development of the cylinder press. It is generally accepted that the first cylinder press was invented by **William Nicholson** of London in 1790. He obtained patents for a machine having the general principles of subsequent designs.

The first really workable cylinder press was patented in 1811 in London by **Frederick Koenig**. Koenig devised a way of moving the printing bed in unison with the cylinder, and introduced composition inking rollers in place of the old inking balls. This press had a flat bed upon which the form was laid and an impression cylinder with three impression surfaces. These impression surfaces were separated by longitudinal grooves in the cylinder.

During the printing operation, the impression cylinder made one-third of a revolution to print during one stroke of the bed and stopped, the bed being returned under the grooves or depressions in the cylinder. The bed was driven by a double-tooth rack and pinion. The pinion was mounted on an arm and was free to move vertically so as to engage both sides of the rack. The arm was connected to its driving shaft by a universal joint. This bed movement is one of the most practical forms still in use, and is known as the mangle rack or Napier movement. Spring cushions were provided for the bed at opposite ends of the stroke. Sheets were fed to the cylinder by means of pins, tapes, or friskets similar to those used on platen presses.

Koenig is also responsible for the invention of the single-stop cylinder press, which substituted tapes for the frisket used on the older presses, and had register racks between the form and the impression cylinder. Both of Koenig's earlier presses were of the stop-cylinder design.

His next improvement was the continuous-revolution machine, in 1814. In this machine, the mechanism which gave the cylinder three intermittent partial rotations for each complete revolution was omitted. Instead, the cylinder was given a continuous rotary movement and was much larger. The impression part of the cylinder was covered with a blanket, the difference in diameter between the blanket-carrying portion and the remainder being sufficient to permit the bed to return while the cylinder was completing its revolution.

The first cylinder press to be made in the United States was built by **Robert Hoe** about 1830 and was of a continuous revolving-cylinder type, making one revolution for each impression. This press had a fly delivery and large coil springs below the bed to absorb the bed-motion shock. At this same time, Hoe made machines known as single small cylinder, double small cylinder, and large cylinder perfecting presses. These presses are manufactured with improvements and alterations to the present day.

The stop cylinder was introduced in France in 1852 by **Dutarte**. On this machine the impression cylinder is of small diameter and is provided with an independent register tooth to actually start and stop the cylinder. The sheet is fed to the cylinder while it is in a stationary position. The cylinder then turns to print the impression and stops again to deliver the sheet and allow the press bed to return under the stationary cylinder. This press was introduced in 1853 to the United States by **Hoe**, who made many improvements.

By this time, the cylinder printing machines had begun to assume the proportions and capabilities of the modern press. For the next 50 years, improvements were made by other inventors, including **Kidder**; **Taylor**, with a bed air-cushioning device; and **Cottrell**, with a bed slider mechanism, the shifting tympan of the second cylinder of the perfecting press, and a printed-side-up press delivery.

The first press turned out by **Miehle** in 1889 marked a new era in the printing trade. In discussing the advances made by the Miehle press, the International Printing Pressmen's and Assistants' Union, Technical Trade School Correspondence Course, the Development of the Printing Press, pages 10, 11, says:

The Miehle was the first two-revolution press in which the bed was driven in actual synchronism with the cylinder. The driving mechanism in common use on other machines produced a more or less irregular motion of the bed, and consequently, in the older presses it was necessary to depend upon the pressure of the cylinder bearers upon the bed bearers for uniform travel during the impression. Fortunately, this was generally not difficult with the type of printing then in common use.

The Miehle also introduced another immensely important element in the two-revolution press—that of adequate impressional strength. The great importance of this element is apparent when it is realized that without it, perfect synchronous driving of the bed and cylinder is impossible in the case of heavy forms in which margins occur. If the press yields under the impression, there is a tendency to lose motion when the cylinder drops into the margins. That these principles were thoroughly understood by the designers of the Miehle is shown by the perfect proportion of impressional strength with relation to the driving mechanism. This was secured by great simplicity of design and a perfect balance of all parts, making it at once the fastest and easiest running press of its type ever devised. It is, therefore, a striking fact that the perfection of this machine came simultaneously with the production of the halftone plate on a commercial basis. Halftone printing called for more accurate registering of bed and cylinder and far greater impressional strength than was present in any of the older machines. The whole technique of letterpress printing had changed.

The Miehle Printing Press Mfg. Co. began in 1887 and produced only six presses in that year. Now there are two-revolution Miehle presses in use in almost every pressroom. The impressional strength and accurate register of Miehle presses made color process printing practical.

QUESTIONS FOR STUDY AND DISCUSSION

1. Why was it necessary that improvements be made in the hand presses that were used for about 400 years?

2. What three general classes of letterpress are in use today?

3. What is the outstanding characteristic of platen presses?

4. In what principal characteristic do cylinder presses differ from platen presses?

5. What is the outstanding characteristic in which rotary presses differ from cylinder presses?

6. Who is generally credited with the invention of the cylinder press?

7. Discuss some of the improvements made by Koenig.

8. Who was the first user of steam power for printing presses in England? In the United States?

9. What improvements were made by Cowper and Applegath?

10. Who was the first manufacturer in the United States to make cylinder presses?

11. What was Dutarte's contribution to the development of cylinder presses?

12. Name some of the later inventors who improved the cylinder presses.

13. What advantages does the Miehle have?

14. What features of the Miehle press made process printing practical?

CHAPTER 11

The Development of Rotary Presses

SUBJECT OUTLINE

A. Some notable names in the development of rotary presses:
   1. Nicholson.
   2. Didot.
   3. Cowper and Applegath.
   4. Hoe.
   5. Bullock.
   6. Marinoni.
   7. Tucker.
   8. Cromwell.

B. Important uses of web presses:
   1. Newspaper printing.
   2. High-grade magazine work.
   3. Jobs which require rewinding after printing.
   4. Color printing.
   5. Process printing.

The original idea for a rotary printing press is accredited to **William Nicholson**, who was also the inventor of the first cylinder press. In 1790 he took out a patent which described a rotary-style machine having the type imposed on a cylinder which was placed between the top inking cylinder and the bottom impression cylinder. The new method of inking was a fine idea. The type to be used with this machine was cast in a wedge shape and set directly onto the cylinder with the narrow end of the type toward the cylinder.

Further improvements contained in the patent by Nicholson were the use of grippers on the impression cylinder to retain the sheet while it was being printed, cylindrical inking rollers to replace the old hand-inking methods, and a power-driven press instead of the hand-operated machines then in use. These patents were indefinite and incomplete, and only the ideas were ever used. In fact, Nicholson was not a mechanic, and none of his ideas were ever put into operation by him.

In the year 1795, an employee of **Didot**, who was a famous Parisian printer, invented a method of casting printing plates from lead matrices. Didot adopted the name "stereotype," which is derived from the Greek words "stereos" meaning solid and "typos" meaning model or image.

In England, Cowper obtained a patent for curving stereotype plates to fit the cylinder of the press, in 1815. The first rotary press was made by **Cowper** and **Applegath** in 1816 and stereotypes were used. In 1848 they developed a rotary press for use in printing the London Times. The type was placed in a large upright central cylinder which was surrounded by impression cylinders.

While the idea in the rotary press field is to print from cylindrical surfaces, this was not completely true of the Applegath machine of 1848, as the cylinder holding the type was composed of a series of flat surfaces. In this machine it was composed of eight surfaces to form a polygon. The machine was capable of producing 8,000 sheets an hour, which represented a great increase over other kinds of printing press.

The sheets were fed to the machine from eight feedboards located above and around the vertical type-carrying cylinder. These sheets were fed to tapes, and grasped by other tapes, and passed sidewise between the type and the impression cylinders. After being printed on one side only, they were removed by the flyboys located beneath the feeding platforms.

The increase in production was not in proportion to the number of cylinders used. Applegath made improvements on this press and produced later models. One of the chief objections to the use of vertical cylinders was the fact that ink collected at the bottom of the printing cylinder, the type being overinked at this point. These presses were soon outmoded by the machines which incorporated the inventions of an American, Richard Hoe.

In 1847 Hoe invented the true type-revolving machine. The type was held on the central form cylinder by means of wedged-shaped column rules, and ordinary type was used. The rules were held to the cylinder by means of grooves. About one-fourth of the central cylinder was used to hold the form, the remaining portion being used as an ink-distributing plate. This machine had four impression cylinders surrounding the form cylinder and was fed sheets which were printed on one side only.

Machines with 6, 8, and later on 10 cylinders were made by Hoe, and production increased from 4,000 an hour on the first press of this kind to 20,000 on later models. The sheets were fed to the press from flat feedboards, with one feedboard for each impression cylinder. These sheets were printed on one side only, but the printed sheets were delivered by tapes and flysticks to a delivery board, which dispensed with the need of a flyboy for each printing cylinder. These presses, though cumbersome, attained world-wide recognition and were supreme in the newspaper printing field for more than 20 years. Despite the ingenious method of holding the type on the form cylinder, numerous accidents occurred, in which type was thrown in all directions from the type-revolving cylinder.

The first efforts to print from a web or continuous roll of paper were made by William **Bullock**, an American who built his first machine in 1865. He was killed a year later by being mangled in the gears of this machine. This press employed a small cylinder to which curved stereotype plates were attached, and the paper was fed from a roll, cut into sheets, and then printed. It operated at a speed of 10,000 impressions an hour. The drawbacks were in delivering and handling the sheets throughout the printing process. It might be said that this press revolutionized newspaper printing, as it was the first attempt to print from a roll of paper. This idea had been advanced earlier, but the art of papermaking had not advanced sufficiently up to this time to fill the need. After Bullock's death, his invention was purchased and developed further by Hoe. Modern high-speed printing was now on its way.

In Paris, **Marinoni** developed a machine with cylinders of equal size which delivered the perfected sheets to separate flyboys in an attempt to speed delivery.

Web printing at this time was being delayed by difficulties such as the sheet offsetting on the second impression, inferior paper rolls, and inadequate delivery of the finished sheet. Many methods and patented ideas were tried in an effort to overcome these faults. Sheets coming from the press on tapes were shuttled to two separate runways, two sheets arriving at the fly-delivery point at the same time and being delivered together by the fly-delivery board. This method was the result of a patent taken out by Hoe and **Tucker** in 1872.

When improvements were made in papermaking, the rotary method proceeded by leaps and bounds, as paper of poor quality had long been a drawback. Improvements for cutting the printed sheets were made by Hoe, inkmakers developed faster drying inks, and a simple folder was used by Hoe in 1875.

The application of another of Tucker's innovations solved many of the delivery problems. A number of sheets were collected, pasted, folded, and delivered, by use of a single cylinder. Both the press and the folder were driven by steam. Toward the end of the century, these high-speed machines were delivering collected and pasted copies at full speed. All that remained to be done after delivery from the machine was the trimming, which was handled by the bindery. On rough work even this was not necessary.

In 1883 Cromwell perfected a new folder by using folding rollers and a device known to newspaper pressmen as the cowcatcher, named after the railroad device it resembled. By this time rotary presswork had reached maturity and all that remained to increase production was to provide more printing units for the individual folder. By this method, the larger newspapers simply added to or subtracted from the number of printing units needed to meet the requirements of any specific edition of the paper.

Let us now consider the **important uses** for which the web press has been designed. Some of the **larger newspaper presses** will print up to 75,000 copies an hour in practically any combination from 4 to 64 pages. Newspaper press units each print 8 pages. If eight press units were operating, the issue size would be 64 pages. The invention of the auto-paster, which automatically attaches a fresh roll of paper, eliminates the necessity of stopping the press to change rolls. Modern rotary presses can print, paste, or stitch, and produce fine work at high speed. A trip to an up-to-date newspaper office is an education to an apprentice and a never-to-be-forgotten experience for the layman.

Besides their outstanding importance as newspaper machines, web presses are also used for **high-grade magazine work.** Food wrappers, oiled tissues, and odd-surfaced papers are also handled on web presses.

Jobs which **require rewinding after printing,** such as theater tickets, streetcar tickets, labels, stickers, fruit wrappers, etc., may be printed on special rotary presses in any number of colors.

Process printing on a large scale also is handled by rotary-style presses, although much of it is done on cylinder machines. This is a complicated subject and an art in itself. Only black and the three primary colors, yellow, red, and blue, are used. These colors are over-printed, that is, printed one on top of the other in various densities to produce any known color or shade.

Modern rotary presses used for process color work, whether letter-press or offset, are similar in construction in that separate printing units are added to print the colors in succession. Modern rotary presses that produce process work via the roll-fed method or web are usually built with four or five plate cylinders about one large impression cylinder. This prints one side; the web is reversed and passed through a similar unit on the opposite side. Register and compensation are generally controlled by an electric eye.

Perhaps a few words should be said about wrap-around plates. Much experimental work has been done in this field in recent years. The wrap-around plate is as the name implies a plate that wraps around the cylinder. It is held in place by clamps at the grippers and a reel or clamps at the other end. Experiments have been conducted with plates made of many materials such as metal and rubber. These plates reduce the imposition time and cost of the many small plates, but as yet the quality, cost and stage of development have restricted their use.

QUESTIONS FOR STUDY AND DISCUSSION

1. Who is credited with originating the idea for rotary presses?

2. Describe the kind of rotary press visualized by Nicholson.

3. What does the word "stereotype" mean? Who was the first printer to adopt this term?

4. Who were the first actually to manufacture a rotary press? Where was it used?

5. Describe the rotary press built by Cowper and Applegath.

6. What were the outstanding features of the rotary press manufactured by Hoe in 1847?

7. Who was the first to manufacture a machine to print from continuous rolls of paper?

8. What difficulties were encountered in early web printing?

9. What innovations did Tucker introduce?

10. What were Cromwell's contributions to the construction of the web press?

11. Discuss the important phases of printing for which the web press is specially suitable.

CHAPTER 12

Preparing Type Forms for Press

SUBJECT OUTLINE

A. Two principal kinds of type forms:
1. Small type forms prepared on the stone:
   a. Clean the stone.
   b. Prepare back of form.
   c. Check quoins.
   d. Examine type.
   e. Check alinement of pages.
   f. Unlock form.
   g. Measure halftone cuts.
   h. Check position of quoins.
   i. Check margins.
   j. Notice kind of type.
   k. Check placement of wood and metal furniture.
   l. Card the form.
   m. Card the quoins.
   n. Plane the form.
2. Larger type forms prepared on bed of press.

B. Precautions to be observed when preparing forms.

All type forms come from the Composing Division locked in chases. The **two principal kinds of type forms** to be considered today are: The small type forms which may be prepared upon the stone tables provided for that purpose in the pressroom, and the larger chases and forms which are prepared directly on the bed of the press.

Let us discuss first the **preparation of a small type form on the stone.** Before the form is placed on the stone, the **face of the stone should be carefully cleaned** with a rag soaked in Varsol and all foreign matter removed.

The next step is to **prepare the back of the form** by scraping it to free it of all burrs or small pieces of type. Then it should be wiped carefully with a rag that may be either dry or soaked with Varsol to remove any remaining dust or dirt.

Before the form is lifted to the stone, precaution must be taken that **all quoins are tight.** This is necessary to prevent any pieces of type from falling from the form when it is lifted.

After the form has been placed on the stone, the **type should be examined** for broken areas and for poor justification. If the justification is poor, the lines of type will be of unequal length and some of the type may be moved with the fingers while the quoins are locked. Sometimes when it is possible to move the type in a locked form it may be because a rule in the form is too long.

If the form contains more than one page, the **alinement of pages** should be checked.

When this preliminary examination has been made, the **form is unlocked** to prepare it for press. To do this, a quoin key of the T-type is used. The quoins in use in the Office are beveled pieces of metal with gear teeth on both sides into which the quoin key fits. When the quoins are tightened they expand to hold the type within the chase.

After the quoins have been loosened, if it is necessary to move the type, this should be done very carefully to avoid dislodging small pieces of type from their position in the form. If there are any **half-tone cuts** mounted on wood blocks within the form, they should be removed and measured by the type-high gage to make sure they are the proper height; but for the time being let us assume that this is a solid type form, without halftones.

The **position of the quoins** should be checked. When type forms are being locked within the chase, the quoins should drive to the solid side. The form is locked on two sides of the chase by the use of quoins, the other two sides of the form being solidly blocked with furniture against the chase. When the quoin nearest the type is in its correct position, its narrow or pointed end is always headed toward the solid lockup. Some of these small chases have a type line scribed or cut in the edge of the chase. As a rule, the form should not extend beyond this line.

The **margins of the job** to be printed should also be checked to see that the type does not extend beyond the scribed type line. Usually it is best to have the form centered as much as possible, but sometimes, because of the size of stock to be printed, this may not be the best procedure. This will be discussed more in detail when the platen makeready process is studied.

The **kind of type** should be considered. If it is monotype, the form will be composed of individual pieces of type; if it is linotype, long lines or slugs of type will be used; and if it is ludlow, the type will be similar to linotype slugs, but will have much heavier faces.

Both **metal and wood furniture** are used. Pieces of metal furniture should not be used in direct contact with the chase, the form, the quoins, or each other. Furniture should always be arranged so that a piece of wood furniture is placed next to any metal.

If the quoins come in contact with any metal, reglets should be inserted between the quoins and the metal. Reglets are small pieces of wood about 3 inches long and about one-twelfth of an inch thick.

The next step is **carding the form**. The purpose of carding is to prevent workups which sometimes occur when type forms are being printed; or pullouts, when poorly justified type is pulled from its place within the form by the impression of the press. Workups may be caused by the form being locked too tightly in the chase, causing the chase to spring; the chase may be warped, in which case it should be replaced; the furniture within the chase may be warped and should be replaced; the furniture may not be true, that is, it may be larger at the top than the bottom; the cuts may be warped, not square, or poorly underlaid; the type may have foreign matter under it, or it may be porous and there may be too much oil in the form or on the bed of the press; or the form may not be properly justified. Whenever a form is poorly justified, a compositor should be called to rectify this condition.

The proper carding of a form takes more time than most pressmen like to allow, but a form which is properly carded will prevent workups that may necessitate long delays while the press is running.

Stock similar to postal-card stock is cut into long strips about one-fourth of an inch wide. These strips are placed next to the type between the form and the adjoining furniture, extending all the way to the bottom of the type. This is done on all four sides of the type form.

Sometimes type pages have been tied up for permanent use and still have the strings wrapped around them. The method of carding forms when the pages are tied will be discussed later.

It is also wise to **card the quoins** themselves by placing cardboard the same height and length as the quoins between them and the furniture.

When the carding is completed, the quoins are made finger tight, starting with those nearest each of the two solid sides of the lockup, and working toward the open corner.

The form is now **ready to be planed** if the face is free from all foreign matter or dirt. The planer is a block of wood with a level face about 10 inches long, 3 inches wide, and varying from 1½ to 2 inches high. The sides are indented to fit the fingers, and the top of the planer is covered with a thin piece of leather which prevents damage to the planer and the type.

The mallet is usually made of leather, composition, or rubber. It has two faces, with the head mounted on a wooden handle about 10 inches long, and weighing approximately 1 pound. If the leather on the planer or the mallet becomes so worn that battered pieces are dropped on the form, it should be replaced.

To plane the form, lay the level face of the planer firmly on the part of the form nearest the solid lockup, and tap the planer lightly but firmly with the mallet. As the planer is moved to other positions on the form, it should be carefully lifted and replaced, until the entire form has been planed.

The quoins should then be tightened slightly by using the quoin key, and the planing process repeated. The quoins are then tightened firmly and the form is ready to go to press.

The procedure of **preparing larger type forms on the bed of the press** is similar to that followed when the form is prepared on the stone. The flat bed of the press is carefully wiped, and a light coat of oil is distributed on the press bed and smoothed over with a rag to prevent rusting.

Details of the method of locking chases on the bed of larger presses will be discussed in the following chapter.

Certain precautions should be observed when type forms are being prepared. Do not allow metal surfaces to come together; always have the quoins driving toward the solid side; be sure the face of the planer is clean and free from grit, and when storing it, place it on its side rather than on its face; never slide the planer on the face of the type, but lift it when moving it from place to place on the form; and do not tighten quoins so tightly as to spring the chase.

Care in preparing the type form for press will prevent many difficulties and much loss of time while the press is running.

QUESTIONS FOR STUDY AND DISCUSSION

1. In this lesson, what two kinds of type forms are considered?
2. When preparing forms on the stone, why is it necessary that the stone and the back of the form should be cleaned?
3. Before the form is lifted to the stone, what precaution should be taken to prevent type being dislodged?
4. Why should the face of the type be examined carefully?
5. If the form contains more than one page, what check should be made?
6. What tool is used to check the height of mounted halftones?
7. What is the correct arrangement of quoins in a form?
8. Why are margins checked?

9. Of what two materials is furniture made?

10. Describe the process of carding a form.

11. What are some of the causes of type workups?

12. What is a type planer? What is a type mallet?

13. Describe the procedure used in planing a form.

14. What additional preparations are made before a form is placed in the bed of a press?

15. Discuss the precautions which should be observed in the preparation of type forms for the press.

CHAPTER 13

Placing Type Forms on the Press

SUBJECT OUTLINE

A. Placing type forms on platen presses:
   1. Preparing the press.
   2. Lifting form from stone to press.
   3. Positioning the chase.
   4. Final inspection.
B. Placing type forms on vertical presses:
   1. Removing feedboard.
   2. Preparing the press.
   3. Lifting form from stone to press.
   4. Placing chase in the press.
C. Placing type forms on cylinder presses:
   1. Positioning the sheet.
   2. Setting the press guides.
   3. Preparing the press.
   4. Positioning the form.
   5. Locking chase to the bed of the press.
D. Safety precautions.

The preparation of type forms for the press was discussed in the preceding chapter and now the procedure for placing these forms on the press will be considered.

When forms are correctly placed on the press, makeready time and the number of mechanical adjustments required are reduced. Incorrectly placed forms result in workups during the press run and necessitate adjustments to insure proper delivery of the sheets. Careful imposition saves the pressmen much makeready and running time.

Placing type forms on platen presses will be discussed first. Type forms for platen presses should be centered as nearly as possible in the chase, but should not be above the center line of the platen. The reason for this will become clear as we progress in the study of platen presses. The type material should be placed so that the platen or tympan will accommodate the whole sheet to be printed. The quoins should be toward the top of the chase and away from the guide edge of the sheet, except in rare instances where this is impossible.

When the form is ready, the **press is prepared** to receive it by running the machine under power or turning it by hand until the form rollers are at their lowest point of travel. When the press is in position, the power should be shut off. The bed of the press is then cleaned with Varsol and treated with a thin film of oil to prevent rust. The impression lever is placed in the forward or off position.

When the pressman **lifts the form from the stone,** he should be sure that the quoins are at the top of the chase and that the printing surface of the form is toward his body. On some platen presses the form is placed on the press from the right side, away from the fly-wheel; but on some others the feeder attachment is on the right side of the machine, and it is necessary to place the form from the flywheel or left side of the press. The form may be balanced on either the side arm or flywheel of the press, with the lower edge of the chase resting on the machine. The pressman can now raise the chase from this position and place it in the bed of the press, standing with his feet apart and balancing himself well. The lower edge of the chase should go behind the bottom lugs on the press bed. The printing surface of the form must not be damaged by contact with any part of the machine, and care must be exercised to avoid hitting the rollers with the lower edge of the chase.

After the form is on the bed of the press, the **chase is positioned** by being held in place with one hand, the chase clamp lifted with the other hand, the chase pushed flat against the bed, and the clamp released. The chase clamp is located at the top of the press bed directly under the ink disk. On some presses, the chase is pushed toward the left side of the bed by the use of a screwdriver as a wedge, and in long runs it is best to hold the chase in place with either a wooden wedge or paper wads. On other presses, a screw through the right press bearer is used to shove the form to the extreme left side of the bed.

A **final inspection** should be made to see that the chase is properly placed behind the bottom lugs and held securely by the top clamp. Tap the top of the chase lightly with a wrench to seat it properly, and check the grippers which should be clear of all the type matter contained within the chase.

Next to be considered is the placing of **type forms on vertical presses.** Locking up for the vertical press presents some complications. The vertical chase is marked with small circles at the bottom which show where the grippers on the press fall in relation to the type to be printed. The side of the chase is marked with a type line and a paper line. The type form should be positioned to correspond to these grippers and margin marks. No part of the form should extend beyond the type line on the chase where it would be subject to damage from the grippers. The paper line on the chase is used to maintain the proper gripper margin for printing.

The procedure in placing a form in the vertical press is somewhat similar to that for the platen press. Removal of the transfer table is necessary only when placing heavy forms in the press bed. The **feedboard is removed** by first running the press to a position where the cylinder is at the top of its travel and the delivery fingers have just begun to move away from it. The rectangular lock at the left side of the feedboard is pushed to the left until it frees itself from the end of the metal front of the feedboard; the left side of the board is raised to an angle of about 45 degrees; and the board is removed from the machine and placed in the brackets at the top of the press frame, directly over the cylinder.

The **press is now prepared** by positioning it with the cylinder at its lowest point of travel, and as a safety precaution the power is shut off from the control box. The bed of the press should be cleaned with Varsol and a light film of oil applied. This is also a good time to clean the bed bearers.

Before the form is **lifted from the stone**, check to be sure that none of the printing matter extends beyond the type deadline. The form is lifted in the same manner as for platen presses, the printing surface being toward the pressman and the quoins uppermost when possible. Exercise care to avoid damaging the printing material.

The **chase should be placed in the press** with the beveled lower edge on and behind the chase jacks, which are two adjustable screws located about one-fourth of the way in from each bed bearer. The form is held with one hand and the top clamp is lifted by using the pin wrench. Then the form is pushed against the bed of the press and the clamp released. As on the platen presses, the chase is moved to the left of the bed by the use of a screwdriver as a wedge. The top of the chase is tapped with the pin wrench to seat it firmly. The paper marks on the chase and on the bed bearers should be alined by the use of chase jacks. While the cylinder is in its uppermost position, these jacks may be turned with either the small pin wrench or a nail set.

And now we come to the discussion of **placing type forms on cylinder presses**. Lockup for the cylinder press is not complicated. The type should be placed in the smallest chase appropriate for the job, and the type material should be centered in the chase.

The method of placing forms on the bed of the cylinder press differs from that used on the platen and vertical machines. The **sheet is**

positioned in regard to the grippers, stripper fingers, shooflies, delivery tapes, and sticks. If these mechanical parts are properly positioned, it is seldom necessary to move them. If an automatic feeder is to be used, the sheet is centered as nearly as possible on the feedboard. However, the sheet must be placed in a position which is both convenient and comfortable when hand feeding is necessary. The distance from the left edge of the sheet to the inner edge of the cylinder bearer is measured, as this measurement is needed in positioning the form on the press bed.

The proper method of **setting the press guides** will be discussed more in detail later. The bottom guides should be placed about one-fourth of the way in from each edge of the sheet to balance it; the side guide is placed from one-third to one-fourth the distance from the gripper edge of the sheet.

The **press is now prepared** by moving its bed to the farthest point of travel toward the back or feeder end, and shutting off the power at the circuit breaker. The bed of the press is cleaned and oiled and the form is placed on the bed of the press, with the gripper edge toward the press clamps.

The next procedure is to **position the form** to the deadline scribed on the press bed. The deadline gage is a handy piece of equipment, but for the present we shall use a sheet of the stock to be printed as a gage. At no time should any of the printing matter extend beyond the deadline. The correct margin should be marked on one edge of a sheet of stock and the sheet placed on the form, with the margin mark alined with the corresponding part of the form. The form is now moved onto the bed of the press until about ¼ of an inch of paper extends beyond the deadline. As the deadline marks the extreme ends of the grippers in relation to the form, this means that about ¼ of an inch of the sheet will extend under the grippers during printing.

The correct amount of furniture to be placed back of the chase must be determined by good judgment and common sense. As few pieces of furniture and blocks of metal or wood as possible should be used. It is good practice to place a piece of 2-pica furniture on its side directly back of the chase. This insures that the chase will be held to the bed of the press.

The form is now ready to be adjusted sideways, either by centering it on the sheet or by using the proper known margin. It will be remembered that, in a previous step, the distance from the edge of the sheet to the edge of the cylinder bearer was measured. This same distance is now measured from the edge of the press bearer to the left edge of the sheet positioned on the form.

After the form has been properly placed, the chase is locked to the bed of the press by means of press clamps. There are four of these clamps. While they are all needed on large forms, generally only the two center clamps are used on small forms. Before the clamps are tightened, the quoins within the chase must be loosened. If the clamps are set too tightly, the chase will be sprung. It is not usually necessary to lock the form sideways between the bearers except for long runs or close-register work. When it must be locked, a piece of 2-pica furniture, laid flat, may be used against the chase. The press should never be run with any of the clamps loose, as vibration may cause them to drop off and do serious mechanical damage. Sometimes it is necessary to lock the chase on the bed with the clamps and then hold it to the clamps by using quoins back of the form.

Safety precautions to be observed while placing forms in or on presses include the following: Be sure to have the power shut off before a form is placed on a press. In lifting, maintain balance and exert the muscles in the legs rather than those in the back. When a form is being placed on a platen or vertical press, the pressman should tense the stomach muscles before lifting the form. Guard against injury to the hands which might result if they are caught under the chase or between the chase and the press, or if the quoin key slips while the quoins are being tightened or loosened. Avoid damage to the form while placing it in the press. Be alert to avoid damage to the rollers while forms are being placed on platen presses.

QUESTIONS FOR STUDY AND DISCUSSION

1. In what position should type forms be placed in chases for platen presses?

2. What preparations are made on the press before the form is lifted from the stone?

3. Describe the process of lifting a form to the bed of a platen press.

4. What procedure is followed in positioning a form in the bed of a platen press?

5. How are vertical chases marked to facilitate the placement of forms in the chase?

6. How is the feedboard of a vertical press removed?

7. What press preparations are made before the form is lifted to the vertical press?

8. Describe the work involved in placing a form on the vertical press.

9. Discuss the proper positioning of a form on a vertical press.

10. By what means is the sheet correctly positioned on a cylinder press?

11. How are the press guides set on a cylinder press?

12. What press preparations are made before a form is lifted to the bed of a cylinder press?

13. Describe the procedure involved in correctly positioning a form on a cylinder press.

14. By what means is a chase locked to the bed of a cylinder press?

15. Discuss the safety precautions which should be observed in placing forms on the press.

CHAPTER 14

Press Imposition of Plate Forms

SUBJECT OUTLINE

A. Factors to be considered before imposing plates:
   1. Number of pages in signature.
   2. Method of binding:
      a. Saddle-stitching.
      b. Side-stitching.
      c. Machine sewing.
      d. Perfect binding.
   3. Fold of the sheet:
      a. Work-and-turn forms.
      b. Sheetwise forms.
      c. Work-and-tumble forms.

4. Kind of base.
B. Method of positioning plates:
   1. Make dummy.
   2. Determine width of margins.
   3. Allow for gripper bite.
   4. Mark center line.
   5. Adjust plate catches or locks.
C. Importance of guide marker.

Several factors are to be considered when plate forms are being imposed on the press. It is necessary that the **number of pages in the signature**, and the **method of binding** be known.

The method of binding a book is influenced by its size, the kind of cover, and the use to which it is to be subjected. Books are made up of signatures of 4, 8, 12, 16, 24, 32, 48, or 56 pages. Saddle-stitching is generally used when there are no more than 6 signatures of 16 pages each. When a book is saddle-stitched it is stitched through the fold, opening flat in the middle. Such books may be either self-covered or have a cover of different stock.

Side-stitching is used when a book has too many pages to be saddle-stitched, but is not more than 1⅛″ thick. When too thick to be side-stitched or when a flat opening is required, books **are sewn by machine**.

The **fold of the sheet** should be considered when a form is to be imposed. Various folds and plate layouts are used. Sixteen printed pages may be run as a **work-and-turn form**, the sheet being printed on one side, turned over, the same form and bottom guides used, and the sheet printed on the reverse side. Thus two copies of the same 16-page form will be printed on each sheet.

A signature may also be run **sheetwise**, the sheet being printed on one side by the use of one form, and then on the reverse side with a second form. If two 16-page forms are used, the sheetwise method will produce a 32-page signature.

Another method which is not used so frequently is known as **work-and-tumble**. This method prints the same form on both sides of the sheet. One disadvantage of the work-and-tumble form is that the paper on which it is printed must be squared by the cutter before it is run off on the press, because one edge is run to the guides when the first side is printed, and on the back-up the other edge is run to the guides.

Bases of various kinds may be used on which to impose the form in the pressroom. One of these is a patented base with diagonal grooves which hold the plate catches. Another kind of base is composed of separate blocks of various sizes, the largest being 8 by 10 inches. The grooves which hold the catches in this base run at right angles to each other and horizontally across the press bed. A third kind of patented base has a series of holes to hold the plate catches. The bases should always be kept clean and free from ink and paper dust to insure proper height of plates and accurate movement of the plate catches. They are usually cleaned with a brush and gasoline, and a light film of oil is applied to prevent rust.

When forms are to be imposed, a book printed for and by the Government Printing Office entitled "Layouts for Imposition" should be used. You will find, however, that through repeated use of some lays you will memorize them and the book will not have to be brought out each time.

If bleed jobs or other production problems necessitate use of an imposition not in the book, a dummy or stone lay will be found in the work jacket. A dummy is used in lieu of the layout book in most outside shops where the workload does not warrant the printing of a book for imposition layouts.

To make up a plate form of bookwork several things need to be known before starting and they can be found on the work jacket or from the supervisor: the imposition code or lay number, sheet size, number of pages, and margins are all essential information. Note the code layout number and lay the plates on the base according to the sequence found in the imposition book under that lay number.

When placing the plates on the base, position the heads in the same relative position as the numbers shown in the layout book. The plates are then to be balanced on the base according to sheet size and margins. On some presses, like the Miehle Vertical and Horizontal, type lines are drawn on the base and of course the plates will always be placed behind these lines in order to avoid hitting them with the grippers.

Center the sheet size on the base to be used parallel to the gripper line, and line up the first row of plates behind the type line. Position them exactly by using the known margins and sheet size, and lock them in place with the plate catches. Next position one of the center rows of plates from front to back, again using the known margins and sheet size, and lock them in place. The remaining plates can be lined up using the parallel lines on the base.

Six catches are used to hold each plate, two on each of the long sides, and one at each end. On the long side a catch is placed about 1 inch from each end of the plate, and on the short side the single catches are centered as nearly as possible. On forms with heavy halftone coverage it is common practice to use one extra catch at each of the ends.

Before pulling a sheet, check to be sure that the edges of the plates do not extend beyond the deadline on the bed of the press and inspect the base to see that no loose catches or pieces of equipment have been left on it.

After an impression has been pulled, the margins are again checked and the sheet folded. The pages should run in rotation. After satisfying yourself that it is all right, it should be sent to the desk for O.K. before sending it in to the reviser for lineup.

A guide marker should always be used on the guide edge of the sheet. The use of the guide marker is very important and should never be neglected, as it is also helpful in the bindery where it is used as a guide edge by the folding-machine operator.

QUESTIONS FOR STUDY AND DISCUSSION

1. Name several factors to be considered before plates are imposed on the press.
2. Describe the saddle-stitching method of binding.
3. When is side-stitching preferable?
4. When a book is too thick to be side-stitched, what method is used?
5. What is a work-and-turn form?
6. Describe the sheetwise method of printing.

7. How does a work-and-tumble form differ from a work-and-turn?

8. How many plate catches or locks are used for each plate?

9. Why is an impression pulled and sent to the reviser?

10. Why is it important to use a guide marker?

CHAPTER 15

Printing Inks

SUBJECT OUTLINE

A. History of printing inks.
B. Definition of term "printing ink."
C. Manufacture of ink:
    1. Weighing.
    2. Mixing.
    3. Grinding.
    4. Testing.
    5. Canning and packaging.
D. Raw materials.
E. Types of printing inks:
    1. Letterpress or typographic inks:
        a. Newsprint.
        b. Job press inks.
        c. Automatic press inks.
        d. Flatbed cylinder press inks.
        e. Rotary press inks.
        f. Heat-set inks.
        g. Moisture-set inks.
        h. Quick-setting inks.
        i. High-gloss inks.
        j. Metallic inks.
        k. Wax-set inks.
        l. Cold-set inks.
        m. Flexographic inks.
    2. Planographic or lithographic inks.
    3. Intaglio (rotogravure and engraving) inks:
        a. Rotogravure inks.
        b. Engraving (plate) inks.
        c. Die stamping inks.
    4. Miscellaneous inks.
    5. Fluorescent inks.
    6. Safety inks.

There is considerable doubt today as to the origin of printing ink. However, as the forerunner of printing inks was writing ink, and the Chinese were among the first to use them, their claim is usually given priority. These early crude inks consisted essentially of carbon black, usually from the chimney, mixed with animal glue or vegetable oil, and were used principally on cloth, bark, and bamboo.

The Chinese advanced the art of inkmaking to a highly developed state and, during the 11th century, were printing from hand-cut blocks. This was some 400 years before Gutenberg introduced his movable type in Europe.

During these early days, before inkmaking became commercialized, the printer made his own by mixing lampblack into boiled linseed oil, cooking it according to his own secret formula and grinding it in a mortar and pestle.

The commercial ink business did not become established in Europe until the 16th and 17th centuries and, by the middle of the 18th century, it was fast becoming an item of commerce in the American colonies, the first factory having been established by Rodgers and Fowle in 1742.

Prior to the discovery of coal-tar dyes, very little color was used by the printing ink industry. In fact, it has been the development of the synthetic color industry which has enabled the inkmaker and the printer to capture and reproduce the various colors of the rainbow.

The inkmaker has had to keep pace with the rapid developments of the graphic arts. The advent of high press speeds and the development of new printing processes have necessitated the formulation of new and suitable printing inks. Today, linseed oil has been partly replaced with the faster and harder drying synthetic oils, and the development of synthetic resins for use in inks has enabled the inkmaker to formulate inks suitable for printing on almost any surface.

Printing ink, by definition, is an intimate mixture of pigments, varnishes, driers, and, quite frequently, waxy and greasy compounds. This, at best, is only a general definition which needs considerable amplification before it will have any practical value. The ink must have the proper viscosity, length, flow, and tack in order to be suitable for the particular type press and stock on which it is to be used. Each type of press and grade of paper requires an ink possessing different physical characteristics in order to insure proper distribution and correct transfer from the type or plate to the paper. The ink must print sharply and give legible prints of the desired color. It must also dry in a sufficiently short time to permit handling without offsetting or smudging.

The manufacture of printing inks consists of a series of steps as follows: weighing, mixing, grinding, testing, and canning. Each will be discussed briefly.

Considerable care must be exercised when weighing a batch of ink. All the weighings must be accurate and the formula must be followed exactly in order to insure the maintenance of uniformity and good quality. All ingredients listed in the formula must be added. Otherwise, the ink will not perform satisfactorily.

Mixing is the second step in the manufacture of an ink and is the process of thoroughly mixing all the ingredients together to facilitate their grinding. There are two general types of mixing equipment employed in the manufacture of printing inks today. They are the dough or kneading type mixer and the change can type mixer. The dough type machine is best suited for the mixing of large batches and can be used for all types except those having very heavy consistencies. The change can type mixer is capable of mixing any type ink. It mixes thoroughly, rapidly, and handles small or large size batches. It also possesses the added advantage of being able to be easily and rapidly changed from one color to another.

The grinding of an ink completes the dispersion of the pigments in the vehicle. It insures the complete wetting of each individual pigment particle by the varnish and reduces any aggregates to the desired particle size. Grinding is usually accomplished by passing the ink through a three-, four-, or five-roll mill. The principle of all mills is the same; that is, the first roll is set to run at a certain rate of speed and each succeeding roll turns in the opposite direction and at a faster rate. The grinding action is produced by this difference in speed and the pressure between the rolls. As the ink passes through the tightly set revolving rolls, a severe rubbing action is set up which affects the grinding.

All ink should be tested for compliance with quality standards before canning or packaging. Generally, an ink is tested for the following characteristics: fineness of grind, color strength and shade, length, tack, and drying time on the stock upon which it is to be printed.

Small batches of ink are usually packaged directly from the mill. However, all large quantities of ink should have the entire lot mixed thoroughly to insure uniformity before packaging. Liquid inks are packaged in bottles which are filled by one or more of the different type filling machines.

The raw materials or ingredients used in the manufacture of printing inks are generally classified into three main categories: the liquid ingredients or vehicles, the pigment or solid ingredients, and the modifying ingredients such as driers and compounds.

The liquid or vehicular portion of an ink is determined largely by the printing process and the drying system involved. Inks dry by one or more of the following ways: penetration or absorption, evaporation, oxidation, precipitation, polymerization, gelation, and solidification.

The vehicle is that portion of an ink which serves as the dispersing and carrying medium for the pigment particles. It gives flow and followthrough to the ink, enables the pigment particles to be carried through the distribution system of the press, and be transferred and firmly bound to the surface of the paper.

Pigments are the coloring or solid material in inks. They are of two types: mineral and organic. The pigment also supplies the contrast with the background, and it is generally responsible for certain specific properties of the ink such as specific gravity, opacity or transparency, and permanency to light, heat, and other agents. The pigment usually determines whether or not an ink is suitable for offset lithography or any other specific use, like printing butter and meat wrappers.

The modifying ingredients are used to impart special characteristics to the ink. They are usually added to the varnish when it is being cooked or included in the ink formulation. However, some may be added to the finished ink to modify it to meet special conditions that may be encountered on the press.

Driers are the materials which act as catalysts. They increase the rate of oxidation or polymerization of the varnish in an ink, thus changing it from the liquid to the solid state. They usually consist of compounds of lead, manganese, and cobalt called "metallic soaps." Cobalt driers are generally the most active; manganese, next; and lead driers are considered to be the least effective. Lead and manganese are generally more effective when used in combination than when used separately. Usually, 1 to 1½ ounces of drier to the pound of ink are sufficient to impart a drying time of 4 hours or less. However, great care must be exercised in the selection of the type drier to be used in a particular ink. Each formulation must be considered separately as each vehicle has its own special drying characteristics, and a proper balance of driers must be maintained in order to insure proper drying on the paper and stability on the press.

There are three main classes of printing inks: typographic, planographic and intaglio. These correspond to the three divisions of printing.

Letterpress or typographic inks include newsprint inks, job press inks, automatic press inks, flatbed cylinder press inks, rotary press inks, heat-set inks, moisture-set inks, quick-setting inks, high gloss inks, metallic inks, wax-set inks, cold-set inks, and flexographic inks. They are used to print from type, plates, line and halftone cuts, and are made from soft pigments ground in a vehicle composed essentially of heat-bodied linseed oil or synthetic resins dispersed in drying oils.

Newsprint inks are adapted to the very high speed web-fed presses and consist essentially of carbon black dispersed in mineral oil. Generally, they are quite fluid and possess low viscosities, depending on the speed of the press. They dry by penetration and absorption into the paper.

Job presses, of which the hand-fed or machine-fed platens are the most common, print on a wide range of papers. Therefore, it is necessary for job inks to fit all of these different papers as well as the presses. The ink should possess as much body as the stock on which it is to be printed will permit, and it should be as short and buttery in nature as is consistent with satisfactory distribution. The body of these inks preferably should be obtained by the inclusion of as much pigment as possible rather than by the use of a heavier varnish, as this will produce a better working ink. When the ink is intended for the better grades of paper, drying oils and driers must be included in the formulation to insure proper drying.

The automatic presses include the automatically fed presses of the small high-speed types such as the platen, flatbed, vertical, and small rotary. Their speeds vary from 3,500 to 10,000 impressions per hour. Generally, the formulation of automatic press inks should be similar to the job inks, except that they must possess considerably more flow and have softer consistencies to accommodate the higher speeds of these presses.

The flatbed cylinder press is manufactured by several different companies and there are variations of design in each. Although one ink could be formulated which would give fairly satisfactory performance on all models, it has been found by experience that a better class of work is produced when an ink is specially adapted to fit the requirements of each press. Generally, flatbed cylinder press inks should possess more flow and be of a softer consistency than the automatic press inks. The greater the press speed and the larger the printing area, the softer and longer the ink must be. The vehicles of these inks must be carefully adjusted to the grade of paper on which they are to be run to insure proper drying. The inks must be finely ground and contain no abrasive pigments which will wear the plates on long runs.

Rotary presses are also built in a variety of sizes and styles. Here again, the ink must be adjusted to the stock and press in order to obtain satisfactory printing. Rotary press inks must be thinner and longer than those designed for flatbed cylinder presses. They should be of such a consistency that, when thoroughly agitated, they will flow smoothly and slowly from the ink knife. If the stock permits, they may contain a rather high percentage of the nondrying oils, such as rosin or mineral oil, with only a sufficient amount of drying varnish to insure a hard drying ink.

Heat-set inks are considered by many to be the most important development in the ink industry in recent years. They have made it possible to print large numbers of publications in great volume, high speed, and good quality. These inks are successful because special vehicles, composed of slightly plasticized synthetic resins dissolved or dispersed in suitable solvents, are utilized in their formulation. The solvents employed have narrow boiling ranges and possess low volatilities at room temperature. However, they are very fast evaporating at the elevated temperatures which the printed matter is subjected to for an instant directly after printing. Consequently, in this heating, the bulk of the solvents leaves the printed ink film by evaporation, thereby resulting in a film that is dry on the paper.

Moisture-set inks consist of pigments dispersed in vehicles composed of water-insoluble resins dissolved in glycols, which are water-miscible or water-receptive solvents. When the printing is subjected to either steam or a fine mist of water, the water-insoluble resin is precipitated out of solution and binds the pigment firmly to the paper. The diluted solvents are absorbed into the paper and a water-insoluble film of ink remains on the surface.

Quick-setting inks depend upon the nature of their vehicles for their drying speed. Synthetic resins are dissolved in solvents to form pseudo-solutions. The resins are so incompletely dissolved that the solvents, at least partially, leave the ink and penetrate into the stock when printing pressure is applied. The pigment and resins remain on the surface, dry rapidly, and are capable of backup within an hour. However, quick-setting inks, especially the blacks, have relatively poor printability and show more chalking and ruboff than other type inks. They are most effective when used on coated papers.

Production of successful high gloss inks depends primarily on the proper formulation and selection of suitable vehicle components. Ordinary linseed oil varnishes, when used alone, are not adequate because they penetrate and are absorbed rapidly by the paper and, therefore, do not exhibit sufficient flow and leveling after printing.

The successful manufacture and introduction of modified phenolic and phenol-modified alkyd resins paved the way for the rapid development of inks possessing high gloss. The synthetic resins, when used in conjunction with synthetic drying oils and chinawood or tung oil because of their excellent drying characteristics, are the most valuable ingredients of high gloss vehicles. The selection of the correct pigments must be an important consideration if high gloss is to be obtained. It is absolutely essential that they be properly and well dispersed for the achievement of satisfactory results. A combination of lead and cobalt drier has been found to give the best results from the standpoint of gloss and speed of drying.

The porosity, degree of sizing, weight, and type of coating of the paper stock are also factors which contribute to the successful attainment of high gloss. Best results are achieved when papers that are specially coated for gloss inks are used. Generally, papers that have the greatest resistance to the penetration of the ink vehicle produce prints having the highest gloss.

Metallic inks consist of a suspension of fine powders in special vehicles which serve to bind the powders to the surface being printed. These vehicles possess characteristics that allow proper "leafing" to take place, which is necessary for the production of high brilliancy and luster. "Leafing" is achieved when the fine metal powders, which are in the form of flakes, float to the surface of the vehicle and form a continuous film.

The need for a more rapid and efficient method of printing and handling bread wrappers and other printed and waxed papers supplied the required incentive for conducting the necessary research which led to the development of wax-set inks. These inks are usually formulated with a vehicle that is composed of a wax-insoluble resin dissolved in a wax-soluble or wax-miscible solvent. The principle involved is the melted paraffin dissolves or leaches out sufficient solvent from the ink to yield substantially dried films of resin and pigment under the paraffin coating.

Cold-set inks are solid at room temperature. Their formulation consists of pigments dispersed in plasticized waxes. Their use demands heated presses in order to maintain the ink in a fluid condition until it is printed. When the ink is impressed onto the relatively cold paper, it reverts almost instantly to its normal solid state. The chief advantage of these inks is their ability to produce prints that do not smudge or offset. Neither do they skin in the can nor dry on the press. They also yield prints possessing a high degree of definition as the vehicles do not penetrate into the fibers or interstices of the paper.

These inks would undoubtedly enjoy a much wider use today if it were not for the unfavorable economic picture involved in maintaining the complicated heating and cooling devices on the presses. As a result, the process is rarely ever used except for special applications, such as hot-spot carbon and transfer printing.

Flexography is a process of printing which utilizes high-speed roll- or web-fed rotary presses that are designed to print from flexible rubber plates with volatile and fluid inks. It is noted for its economy, versatility, quality, simplicity, and ease of operation. A roll of material can be multicolor printed in a continuous web at speeds up to 700 feet per minute. After printing, the rolls can be either rewound or fed directly into converting or other processing machines.

Although small, single-unit, flexographic presses are known, it is the multiunit high-speed presses that print as many as six colors that are commercially the most important. Each unit of the press consists of the following: ink fountain, fountain roller, form roller, plate cylinder, and impression cylinder. The fountain roller revolves in the liquid ink and, by squeeze contact, transfers and distributes it to the form roller which, in turn, places a thin film on the rubber plates.

Initially, flexography utilized only transparent inks composed of solutions of aniline dyes dissolved in alcohol. However, today more than 80 percent of the inks consumed are formulated with pigments. The vehicles consist of solvents and resins blended together to impart the required rheological properties. The inks are made in a very wide range of colors and shades and are noted for their brilliance of tone.

In addition, there have been developed a series of water-based inks which utilized shellac dissolved in water containing ammonia and borax as the principal ingredient. Concentrated pigment pastes, which are organic pigments highly dispersed in water, are available for use in these inks and it is only necessary to provide a means of simple stirring for their incorporation into finished inks.

Flexographic inks dry principally by evaporation, although in some instances partially by absorption, especially when alcohol is used as the chief solvent.

Flexography is utilized in printing all types of plastic film, glassine, tissue, and other paper stocks. It is also used to decorate aluminum foils, paperboard, and corrugated liners. Its colorful reproductions can be seen almost anywhere on bags, wraps, box coverings, folding cartons, paper cups, gift wrappings, and a multitude of other items.

Planographic printing is the second major process of printing and includes all processes that print from a flat or slightly etched surface, that is, where the image sections are in substantially the same plane as the nonimage sections. Stone lithography, offset lithography, and dry offset are the principal processes. Lithography is the only process of printing in which chemicals and chemistry play a major role. With the exception of dry offset, the fact that oil and water do not mix is the basis for its success. The image that is to be printed is placed upon the printing medium by means of a greasy ink; the nonprinting areas are then wet with water which is repelled by the oiled or printing areas. These wet, nonprinting areas will not accept ink and, consequently, do not print.

Generally, an ink for offset or stone lithography must be very concentrated, as in these processes it is impractical to carry large volumes of ink. This requires that as much pigment as possible be ground into the vehicle as will be consistent within the limits of length, lifting, and gripping qualities imposed by the process. The ink, however, must not be too tacky or it will tear the paper and destroy the printing design on the plate. Water containing small quantities of dilute acids is generally used to dampen the nonprinting areas of the stone or plate and these inks must, therefore, not contain any substance that is soluble in water and dilute acids or that can be easily emulsified with them.

Lithographic inks may contain more than a dozen ingredients to insure satisfactory performance on the press. These include one or more pigments, one or more lithographic varnishes, at least one compound, perhaps an extender, and several driers. The pigments impart the desired color; the vehicles serve as the dispersing and carrying medium for the pigments, giving flow and followthrough to the ink, and permit it to be transferred and firmly bound to the surface of the paper. The compounds impart special properties and the driers change the fluid ink into a solid. In order to improve gloss, impart faster drying, and produce harder and more rub-resistant prints, synthetic varnishes are frequently used as a replacement for the regular drying oil varnishes.

Intaglio is a process of printing from engraved or depressed surfaces. Its most important processes are rotogravure, engraving, and die stamping.

Rotogravure is an excellent method for the fast reproduction of magazine color prints. It produces soft pictures possessing a wide tonal range. The gradations are obtained by controlling the depth of the etch, thus creating a variation in the thickness of the ink film being deposited. The gravure press is probably the simplest printing machine in existence today. It consists essentially of a gravure cylinder on which the design to be reproduced is etched; the impression cylinder which forces the printing web into intimate contact with the gravure cylinder; the doctor blade which removes the excess ink from the surface of the gravure cylinder; and an ink fountain which serves as an ink reservoir.

Gravure inks usually contain only three ingredients: the pigment which imparts color, the various resins which serve as binding agents to hold the ink to the printed surface, and the solvents which act as a carrying medium for the pigment and resins. These inks dry rather fast, chiefly by evaporation, and to some extent by penetration. Drying is usually expedited by the application of heat or airblast.

Engraving is a process that is used for the production of fine stationery, postage stamps, paper money, and illustrations for fine books. The design to be printed is cut, usually by hand, into the surface of a copper or steel plate by an engraver, and requires great skill in its execution.

Engraving inks are generally quite short and buttery in consistency. However, they must be greaseless to permit easy wiping. They must be absolutely free from coarse and abrasive pigments that would cause excessive wear to the plates. Also, pigments that bleed in oil and water cannot be used, as the paper is usually moistened before use and the thick, heavy film laid down on the paper has a tendency to amplify any bleeding of the pigment. The vehicle should consist only of the best grades of burnt or heat-bodied plate oils, properly blended to give the ink its desired characteristics.

Die stamping or die engraving is an intaglio printing process that combines both printing and embossing in one operation.

Stamping and embossing are usually done on a power-embossing press and there are several known makes on the market. They all ink the die, wipe the excess ink off the surface, and make the impression at a speed that compares favorably with that of an ordinary hand-fed press.

There are two general types of die stamping inks: the gloss inks and those that dry with a dull plate finish. The gloss inks are designed for the hard-finished papers, while the dull inks are more suited for the softer and matte-finished stocks. Both inks should have a consistency that will permit sharp printing without, at the same time, being squeezed out of the lines of the engraving. They should, however, be thin enough to distribute properly and wipe easily from the face of the plate. Die stamping inks should have only sufficient length to permit an even flow into the fine lines of the engraving as excessive length will cause them to be drawn out during the wiping process.

The vehicles of the gloss inks should consist almost entirely of the rapid drying, greaseless, and almost tackless gum varnishes. These include gum rosin, synthetic copal, coumarone esters, and the better grades of substitute turpentine. These various gums, resins, and substitute turpentine are melted together and strained to remove foreign matter. Sometimes a little plate oil is added to improve the wiping qualities and toughness of the dried film.

As only limited quantities of drying oils are present, small percentages of driers are sufficient to produce satisfactory drying. The dull inks are all formulated with a flatting varnish, such as a dull drying gum dissolved in substitute turpentine. Only pigments that dry with a flat finish can be used in these inks, and a thin Japan drier will cause the ink to dry to as dull a finish as possible.

In addition to the three major printing processes, there is a small number of other methods that are important in certain specific fields of operations. One of these is the silk-screen process of printing. It is enjoying widespread popularity as a means of decorating glass, china, pottery and porcelain. It is used to print on a wide variety of other surfaces such as metal, canvas, sign cloth, muslin, velour, felt, and plastic.

Silk-screen inks must be short and buttery in order to print sharply and prevent excessive drag on the squeegee. It must also be nonoily; otherwise, oil halos will disfigure the prints. The ink should spread easily over the screen without excessive force and permit the print to drop from the screen without causing blur. The vehicles must not contain any toxic and malodorous materials. They must possess sufficient flow to smooth out the mesh marks and be nonreactive with the stencil-forming materials.

Fluorescent inks are made from conventional materials, except for the pigments which have special fluorescent properties. Fluorescence is the emission of light which continues only when a source of light is present and there is no afterglow.

Fluorescent pigments are of two types: the daylight fluorescent and the "black light" fluorescent. Both types absorb light of a particular wave length and readmit it at a longer wave length. Fluorescent colors are available in a wide range of hues. However, the daylight fluorescent blue is the most difficult to obtain as blue lies in the shorter portion of the spectrum. Formerly, fluorescent inks were suitable for printing only by silk screen and letterpress. However, present-day developments have enabled the inkmaker to produce satisfactory inks for offset, gravure, and flexography.

Safety inks may be described as inks that possess certain special characteristics which enable persons, who are in the "know," to determine the authenticity of or prevent the alteration or counterfeiting of checks and other valuable documents.

A solution of a sensitive aniline dyestuff in a glycerol-dextrin medium serves as one example of a safety ink. Another example, such as is used in check printing, is the inclusion of some colorless chemical in the formulation which will react with the ordinary chemical ink eradicators to form highly colored and fast to light materials when attempts are made to alter any writing thereon.

QUESTIONS FOR STUDY AND DISCUSSION

1. What ingredients were used in the first inks made in China?
2. What development enabled the inkmaker and printer to capture and reproduce the various colors of the rainbow?
3. Name the steps used in the manufacture of printing inks.
4. What is accomplished by the grinding of an ink?
5. What characteristics are checked when testing ink?
6. The ingredients used in the manufacture of printing inks are generally classified into three main categories. Name them.
7. What is the function of driers in ink?
8. What type of pigment, dryer, and paper will generally produce prints having the highest gloss?

9. Name the principal types of letterpress inks and tell how they dry on the sheet.

10. What characteristics are desired and required in lithographic inks?

11. What are safety inks used for?

CHAPTER 16

Rollers for Printing Presses

SUBJECT OUTLINE

A. History:
1. Inking balls.
2. Buckskin rollers.
3. Composition rollers.
B. Ingredients:
1. In early composition rollers.

2. In modern composition rollers:
  a. For winter use.
  b. For summer use.
C. Manufacture:
1. Composition rollers.
2. Nonmelt surface rollers.
3. Solid rubber rollers.

The history of rollers for printing presses, their ingredients, and the method of manufacture are the topics in this chapter. First to be considered is their **history.**

Inking balls were the first method used to ink press forms. These were rounded cushions about the size of boxing gloves, mounted firmly on strong wooden handles and used in pairs. They were made of untanned sheepskin or buckskin carefully chosen to insure fine results. The skins were soaked, curried, and stretched to make them uniformly smooth, carefully stuffed with wool to give the desired shape, and securely fastened to the handles. A small daub of ink was worked between the two inking balls and spread over the surfaces by rocking the two faces together. The ink was then applied by pounding lightly on the forms with the inking balls. This produced excellent results but required much skill and was slow. However, inking balls were used for nearly 400 years, and they have become a symbol of the printer's trade.

The first printing rollers were **buckskin covered** and were more durable than some rollers of today. They were ideal as distributing rollers, but they would not transfer the ink to the form properly, and the seams presented a disadvantage. These rollers were first introduced in 1790. The early rollers were placed in hand racks which were applied directly to the form. Later, two rollers were used in the same rack to provide better ink distribution.

93

The first use of **composition rollers** for printing presses is credited to two Englishmen, Forster and Harrild, in 1810, although they had been used earlier in England to transfer designs to pottery and to the irregular surfaces of dishes. The first composition rollers for printing presses in the United States were introduced by Daniel Fanshaw and Samuel Bingham about the year 1825.

The **ingredients** used in **early composition rollers** were glue and molasses, but they would not be suitable for the high-speed presses in use today, as they were very susceptible to weather and temperature changes. With the addition of glycerin, however, many of the previous reactions to weather conditions were overcome. The use of glycerin in rollers prevents drying and shrinking. Glycerin absorbs moisture, never freezes, and mixes perfectly with water, but it also has its faults. When a roller containing glycerin is subjected to dampness, the glycerin absorbs so much moisture that the roller becomes waterlogged and useless.

Many of these roller problems are eliminated by controlled atmospheric conditions in the pressroom.

The composition rollers in our plant are made the same, year around, because we maintain constant temperature and humidity.

Modern composition rollers are composed of glue, glycerin, sugar sirup, and other ingredients, depending on the manufacturer and the kind of roller needed. Rollers having one part glue to two parts glycerin are used for fast-running web and high-grade flatbed work. Glue, glycerin, and sugar sirups in equal parts produced rollers suitable for common grades of cylinder and job work. Rollers for **winter** use contain **more** glycerin to prevent them from drying out in artificial heat, while those for **summer** contain **less** glycerin to prevent them from becoming waterlogged.

Composition rollers are **manufactured** around a steel core or stock which fits the press for which the roller is being made. This core or stock should be perfectly alined and the spindles fitted on the ends. The core is thoroughly cleaned, and those portions toward the ends of the core which are to be covered by the ends of the roller compound are carefully wound with linen twine. The core between the portions wrapped with linen twine is painted or prepared with adhesive to hold the composition to the core.

The gatling or modern process of making or shooting rollers was invented by Leander Bingham, son of the Bingham who helped produce the first rollers in the United States. The roller gun or mold is made from brass or steel and may contain from 6 to 40 roller molds in the single unit. The molds run lengthwise in the gun and may be of various sizes in a single gun. The cylindrical molds are cleaned and oiled carefully, a thin, even film of sperm or lard oil being applied with a swab. The roller cores are then centered in each mold by means of centerpieces or stars which hold the cores perfectly in the center of the mold. The molds not used are blocked off, and the whole gun elevated to a vertical position and heated.

During this operation, the compound of glue and glycerin has been cooked and prepared and is ready for use. In the actual shooting of the roller, a hose from the composition drum is connected to the mold and the compound is forced into the mold by air pressure. As the compound enters the bottom of each mold and works its way slowly to the top, air bubbles are eliminated. After the molds have been filled, the pressure is stopped and cold water is circulated through the gun. When the cast is cool, the rollers are removed and are ready for seasoning.

Seasoning requires from one day to two weeks and provides the roller with the desired tacky coat. To prevent excessive seasoning, the rollers not used immediately are covered with oil or nondrying ink. The kind of press on which the rollers are to be used governs the amount of seasoning they require. For a slow-running machine, where softer rollers may be used, the seasoning period is shortened; and for faster presses, where harder rollers are needed, the seasoning period is lengthened. Rollers at this time, as always, must be very carefully handled to prevent injury to their surface.

The finished roller should have a perfectly round, true surface, free from pinholes and cuts. The compound must have sufficient tack or adhesiveness to take ink from the ink disk or plate and deposit it on the form.

Rollers to meet the demands of the higher speeds of modern presses have been produced to overcome friction which developed in the old composition rollers and caused them to run down. One roller run down because of too much friction, because of being improperly set, or because the ink used with it was too tacky, can ruin all the rollers in the press and delay production for hours. The roller expands as it becomes heated, and the heating process is stepped up even more. Any roller showing signs of becoming overheated should be removed from the press immediately, as the condition of the press and form may be imagined if the roller melts completely to its original state of glue, molasses, and glycerin.

One kind of roller designed to overcome this condition has a specially prepared **nonmelt surface** about $\frac{3}{32}$ of an inch thick applied over a permanent rubber core. Good results have been obtained with these rollers, but the skin or surfacing is susceptible to damage. It is impossible for these rollers to run down, yet they retain the necessary advantages of the composition rollers. Tannic acid or other chemicals are added to the composition in extra amounts to make these rollers. In appearance and working qualities there is little difference between the nonmelt and composition rollers, but the nonmelt variety retain their tack for a long time and are less subject to atmospheric changes.

The nonmelt surface composition is poured slowly over an under-sized roller core of vulcanized rubber composition. This is done on a patented machine which revolves the roller as the composition is applied. After preparation, the roller must be seasoned. The seasoning process takes only 2 days as compared to the longer period required for other rollers, but it is generally conceded that results obtained are not as good as with composition rollers.

Many kinds of rubber rollers have been tried on letterpress machines but have not been entirely successful. They lack sufficient tack, which causes them to slip over the form while it is being inked, and when the reversing movement is started. Solid rubber rollers have found their place on high-speed web presses where the speed makes composition rollers unusable. The lack of tack in rubber rollers presents no problem in rotary press printing where motion is in one direction and the sidewise motion of the rubber distributor rollers is accomplished by power-driven arms. Solid rubber rollers are also used for watercolor printing. Water has but little effect on them, whereas composition rollers would absorb the moisture and last only a short while. Rubber rollers are also free from the oils and greases found in composition rollers which affect watercolor ink.

If rubber rollers are properly set when first placed in the press and regular inspections and adjustments are made, they should last for years. The inks used on many web presses do not dry between runs; therefore it is seldom necessary to wash the rollers. However, it is sometimes necessary to wash them to remove the dirt and paper dust which collects while the press is running.

Since oil is harmful to rubber, great care should be exercised to keep rubber rollers free from oil. Inks containing oil harm rubber rollers, so Varsol should be used to clean them and the plates from which the printing is done.

Two important advantages of rubber rollers are: They will not shrink as do composition rollers; and, after the surface becomes worn or damaged, they may be reground and the surface repolished to new roller condition. After they are reground, the diameter will be slightly reduced, but that provides no handicap.

Rollers for printing presses are being improved constantly by the use of synthetic materials and continual research.

QUESTIONS FOR STUDY AND DISCUSSION

1. What was the earliest method of applying ink to type forms?

2. What kind of covering was used for the first printing rollers?

3. Where and when were the first composition rollers used for printing presses?

4. Who were the first to use composition rollers in the United States?

5. What ingredients were used in the early composition rollers?

6. What ingredients have been added to modern composition rollers?

7. How are rollers treated to allow for differences in winter and summer temperatures?

8. Discuss the gatling process of making rollers.

9. Why is it necessary to have special rollers for high-speed presses?

10. What kind of rollers are specially designed for high-speed web presses?

11. For what kind of printing are solid rubber rollers specially suitable?

12. What ingredient in some cleaning agents and in some inks is harmful to rubber rollers?

13. What cleaning agent should be used for rubber rollers and the forms from which they are to print?

14. Name two important advantages of rubber rollers.

CHAPTER 17

The Setting and Care of Rollers

SUBJECT OUTLINE

A. Two kinds of inking mechanisms for cylinder presses:
   1. Rack-and-cam or pyramid method.
   2. Table-distribution method.
B. Setting cylinder-press rollers:
   1. Four methods:
      a. Type-high roller gage.
      b. Paper.
      c. Visual.
      d. Contact.

   2. Form rollers to vibrator rollers.
   3. Distributing rollers.
   4. Ductor rollers.
C. Setting platen-press rollers.
D. Marking rollers.
E. Caring for rollers:
   1. Cleaning.
   2. Oiling.
   3. Storing.
   4. Handling.

An important subject, from the pressman's standpoint, will now be considered—the setting of the rollers and their care. This is one of the most important phases of presswork, and a thorough knowledge of how to set rollers will help to avoid printing troubles.

First to be considered are the **two kinds of inking mechanisms** used on cylinder presses. The **rack-and-cam** inking mechanism consists of a **pyramid** of alternating steel and composition rollers. Generally, only two composition rollers known as "form rollers" contact the form on cylinder presses, commonly called "bobtails." On rotary and newspaper presses, however, more form rollers contact the form and better inking is achieved. When this kind of ink distribution is used on short flatbed presses, the form is uncovered and easy of access, and the printed sheets are delivered face up by fly delivery under the feedboard.

The second kind of inking mechanism is known as **table distribution.** In this method, the ink fountain is set some distance from the cylinder, and an extension called the ink table is attached to the bed of the press. This ink table is about the same size as the bed of the press, and its surface is about type high above the bed. Besides the form rollers, which may be two or more in number in this kind of ink distribution, there are usually four distributing rollers which are set at an angle with the ink plate for better distribution. The inking for better kinds of printing is done by this method on standard presses, while cheaper grades of printing are done by the rack-and-cam method on bobtail presses. Either the face-down fly delivery or the sliding face-up delivery may be used. On modern presses, however, the extended pile delivery is used.

The **setting of rollers on cylinder presses** which employ the table style of ink distribution will now be discussed. There are four methods of setting these rollers: the type-high roller gage method, the paper method, the visual method, and the contact method.

When there is no form on the press or only a small form, the form rollers may be set by means of the **type-high roller gage.** The press is then run so that the form rollers are directly over the empty bed of the press or over the empty portion of the bed. The form rollers are moved away from the metal vibrating rollers, and the thumb-screws loosened so that the roller setting may be changed easily. The roller gage is placed between the roller to be set and the bed of the press. First one end of the roller is set, then the other end. When the roller is set to the correct height, it should leave a mark about ¼ of an inch wide on the roller gage. When one roller has been set, the same procedure is followed to set the other form rollers.

The **paper method** of setting the rollers is slow but very effective and must be used in some cases. The rollers are first backed away from the metal vibrating rollers, and the table of the press is run to meet the form rollers. Three sheets of paper are used on each end of the rollers. Two pieces are wide and the sheet which is sandwiched between the two is much narrower. The rollers are raised from the ink table and the sheets of paper are inserted. The rollers are then lowered until proper contact is determined by the drag on the center slip of paper. The form rollers are then set to the metal vibrating rollers.

Form rollers may be set by the **visual method** to either the form or the ink plate. For either of these settings, the form rollers should be moved away from the vibrators. When the rollers are to be set to the form they are raised, and the form is washed and positioned under the form rollers. The rollers are then lowered and allowed to remain in their locked position on the form for a few seconds, then raised and the press positioned so that the marks left on the form may be seen. The roller sockets are raised or lowered until the desired setting is obtained. Rollers are seldom set to the form unless a large form is being printed.

To set the form rollers to the ink plate, they should be moved away from the vibrators, locked in operating position, and the press run until the plate clears the rollers. The form rollers are then raised and the plate positioned under them. From this point on, the same method is followed as that used to set the rollers to the form.

By far the most common method of setting form rollers is by contact with either the form or the ink plate. The form rollers are first freed from the metal vibrating rollers, and the sockets then lowered until the form rollers rest on the ink table or form. The sockets are gradually raised until they lightly contact the roller spindles. A check is then made to see if the proper setting has been achieved.

To set the **form rollers to the vibrators**, the rollers are locked in the operating position over the bed of the press so that they are clear of the form and the ink table. The form rollers may now be moved and set to the vibrators by the use of the visual, the contact, or the paper method.

The **distributing rollers** are set to the ink table by the visual method, the paper method, or the contact method. They are moved away from the metal rollers and then set to the ink table. The distributing rollers are finally adjusted to the metal vibrator rollers while the bed of the press is in its rearmost position.

The **composition ductor roller**, which carries the ink from the fountain for distribution, is first set to the ink table and then placed in its lowest position by moving the press. The fountain is then moved forward or backward until satisfactory contact with the ductor roller is attained. Roller settings on the Miller SY cylinder presses, the Miehle 61 sheet-fed rotary presses and web rotary presses require special instructions. This information can be obtained from the manuals issued by the manufacturer. Copies of the manuals are available for use from the section foremen.

Setting rollers on the platen press is a simple task. The type-high roller gage method is the only practical one to be used for this purpose. The form or inking rollers are held to the inking disk by spring tension and no adjustment is required. Two factors control the height of the rollers from the press bed or form: the press bearers and the diameter of the roller trucks which ride on the bearers. Either one of two sizes of metal trucks may be used, and these are held to the ends of the roller stocks by keyways.

To set rollers on the platen press, run the ink rollers to a position directly over the empty bed of the press, check their height by using the roller gage at both ends of the rollers, and attempt to get a mark

¼ of an inch wide on the gage. If a narrower mark is made, remove the large trucks and replace with smaller ones. If these fail to make the ¼-inch mark, new rollers should be ordered since the old ones have shrunk too much to be of value. If suitable rollers are not available, the form may be underlaid to bring it in proper contact with the rollers. This is an emergency measure, and the small form rollers should be replaced as soon as possible.

When the mark on the roller gage is too wide, several adjustments are possible to raise the rollers from the bed. Trucks of larger diameter may be used, and, if they do not raise the rollers sufficiently, the bearers may be built up by pasting cardboard or paper on them until the desired height is reached, or the circumference of the trucks may be increased by wrapping them with friction tape.

Patented expansion trucks are used successfully in many pressrooms. Each truck consists of a rubber core between two metal collars, one of which is adjustable. As pressure is exerted on the adjustable collar, thus compressing the rubber core between the metal collars, the rubber core is forced outwardly, increasing its diameter. Roller settings exactly as desired thus may be obtained by careful adjustment. Truck and bearing surfaces should be kept clean at all times to insure the friction necessary to turn the rollers over the form. Trucks also are subject to wear, and worn ones should be replaced.

This discussion of setting composition rollers on platen presses concerns only the older machines. The more modern platen presses have other mechanisms which permit the pressman to obtain more accurate roller settings. These adjustments will be dealt with in later chapters.

New composition form rollers should be marked as they are placed in the press. A small nick is cut in the extreme end of the roller on the control side of the press, number one roller being next to the cylinder and the other rollers numbered consecutively toward the ink fountain. The distributing rollers are numbered in the same way. Only composition rollers may be cut on the ends to mark them for position. For all other kinds of form and distributing rollers, a record should be kept of the stock number which is found on one or both ends of the metal core. A check of the rollers should be made every morning before starting the press run. This requires only a few minutes and may save trouble later on. When new rollers are received, the edge should be beveled at each end if this has not already been done.

The first thing to be remembered in the care of composition rollers is that they should always be cleaned with Varsol or oil, neither of which will harm the surface of the roller. Unless ink has been allowed to dry upon the rollers, either Varsol or oil will clean them thoroughly.

If ink has been allowed to dry on the rollers, or if certain colors of ink have been used, it is sometimes necessary to use harsh solvents to clean the rollers. After such harmful cleaners have been used, it is always best to apply oil or nondrying ink to the surface of the rollers. This same treatment should be applied when water is used to clean rollers that have been used to print with copying ink. Ink should never be allowed to dry on rollers. When rollers must be left overnight in the press, or when the cleaning by washup crews may be delayed, it is always best to run a light coat of oil over the rollers. When a small form that does not run the entire length of the roller is to be printed, it is best to run oil or grease on the ends not being used.

When rollers are to be **stored**, they should be coated with either a nondrying ink or oil and placed in a rack in upright position. No part of the roller should touch or lean against any other object.

Care should also be used in **handling** rollers, in order to prevent damage to their surface. When rollers are left in the press for any length of time, the press should be so positioned that they are free of the form, ink table, or any other surface.

Many of the printing troubles sometimes attributed to ink are actually caused by rollers. Among the difficulties which may be caused by rollers are slurs and roller marks, ghosts and shadows, etc. The most common causes of such difficulties are the faulty setting of rollers, bent stocks or uneven distributing surfaces, hard-surfaced rollers, varying circumferences, composition not centered on stock, rollers reversing on the form, and worn roller sockets or driving mechanisms. Some of these faults may be overcome by proper roller setting, while for others replacement or repair of the rollers is necessary.

One development has been the polyurethane roller. Polyurethane rollers are manufactured by casting in molds in a manner similar to composition rollers.

Polyurethane rollers combine many of the desirable properties of composition and rubber. They have good tack and superior printing qualities, are not affected by changes in temperature or humidity, and are extremely resistant to abrasion.

QUESTIONS FOR STUDY AND DISCUSSION

1. Name two methods of distributing ink for cylinder presses.
2. Describe the rack-and-cam or pyramid method.
3. Discuss the table-distribution method.
4. Name four methods by which cylinder-press rollers may be set.

5. Discuss the type-high roller gage system of setting form rollers.

6. How may rollers be set by the paper method?

7. What is the visual method of setting rollers?

8. Describe the contact method of setting rollers.

9. How may form rollers be set to vibrator rollers?

10. How are distributing rollers set to the ink table?   To the vibrating rollers?

11. Discuss the setting of rollers on old models of platen presses.

12. How should composition rollers be marked as they are placed in the press?   Why is this necessary?

13. What solvents should be used to clean composition rollers?

14. If it should be necessary to use harsher solvents on composition rollers, what treatment should follow?

15. In what position should rollers be stored?

16. What precautions should be observed in handling rollers?

CHAPTER 18

Paper

SUBJECT OUTLINE

A. Early writing material:
   1. Papyrus.
   2. Parchment.
   3. Vellum.
B. Invention and development of paper.
C. Fourdrinier papermaking machine.
D. Wood pulp.
E. Rag pulp.
F. Common terms used in connection with paper:
   1. Stock.
   2. Ream.
   3. Substance or basis weight.

G. Kinds of paper generally used in the pressroom:
   1. Newsprint.
   2. Book.
   3. Offset.
   4. Coated.
   5. Bond.
   6. Manifold.
   7. Miscellaneous.
   8. Top sheets.
H. Three outstanding characteristics of paper:
   1. Grain.
   2. Wire side and felt side.
   3. Watermark.

First, the history of paper will be considered briefly. Of the early materials on which writing was reproduced, papyrus was the first of which we have any record. It was prepared and used by the Egyptians about the year 2000 B.C. The word "paper" is derived from papyrus. It is interesting to note that rolls of papyrus, some of them 30 feet long, are still in fair condition though brown and brittle with age. The use of this writing material extended to continental Europe, and the revenue from its export was very great.

Two other especially prepared writing materials were used in the early days. Parchment was made from the skins of sheep or goats, and vellum from the skins of young lambs, kids, or calves.

The invention of paper has been accredited to the Chinese in the year A.D. 105. By a series of wars and other events, the art of making paper spread to other Asiatic countries and to Europe. For centuries the Arabs and Moors were considered the papermakers of the world.

In the 14th century the manufacture of paper was begun in northern Italy, and it was here that all paper used by the early German printers was manufactured. Then it was introduced to England and later to the United States, where production of paper was begun in Germantown, Pa., in 1690, by William Rittenhouse.

In the year 1774, chlorine was used as bleaching agent, making possible the manufacture of white paper from rags which were not white. Shortly thereafter, in 1790, paper having a gloss was manufactured in England. This was accomplished by pressing the paper with a hot surface.

Until about the beginning of the 19th century, all paper was made by hand. In 1798, Louis Robert, of France, invented the **Fourdrinier papermaking machine**, which was first used in England in 1804. The Fourdrinier machine produces paper in its final state after the prepared pulp has been fed to it. The first papermaking machine in this country was operated in 1827, at Saratoga, N.Y.

Wood pulp was first used in 1850 to make the cheaper grades of paper. The wood was boiled in chemicals to soften it and to separate the fibers. After this preparation, the wood pulp was ready for the papermaking machine.

Rag pulp is prepared in the following manner: The rags are cleaned, and all buttons, pieces of metal, and foreign matter removed from them; they are then cut into small pieces and cooked in a bath of caustic soda and lime to clean them thoroughly; these small pieces, which are about an inch or an inch and a half square, are bleached white in a bath of chlorate of lime; the rags are beaten to pulp by machines and the various ingredients added to produce the desired finish; and the pulp is then kept in constant motion until it is used in the Fourdrinier machine.

The pressman should become familiar with the **terms used in connection with paper**. In the pressroom, paper is known usually as **stock**. A **ream** is a unit of quantity of paper, usually 500 sheets; however, a short ream is 480 sheets, and a printer's ream 518 sheets. **Substance** refers to the basis weight of paper or stock, and is determined in the Government Printing Office by the weight of 1,000 sheets of a given size. (In commercial shops the substance is determined by the weight of 500 sheets of a given size.) In this Office, the terms "basis weight" is used interchangeably for substance, while in commercial shops the expression used is "basic weight."

Next to be discussed are the **kinds of paper generally used in the pressroom**. The cheapest of all printing paper is **newsprint**, which is made from wood pulp, and is very soft and absorbent. Newsprint deteriorates rapidly and is therefore used only on publications which are not expected to last long or withstand hard wear. The basis weight for newsprint is figured for sheets size 24 by 36 inches. If 1,000 sheets of this size weigh 64 pounds, the basis weight of that specific grade of paper is 64 pounds.

Many grades of paper, from the cheapest to the more expensive, are known as **book paper.** For all book paper used in the Government Printing Office, the basis weight is determined by the weight of 1,000 sheets size 25 by 38 inches. One grade of book paper is machine-finish, which is made by running the thoroughly dried paper through a stack or calender of chilled iron rollers. These rollers, by pressure, produce machine-finish book paper. This grade of paper is fairly soft and is used for ordinary bookwork and also for filler sheets in soft packings or tympans. Coarse halftones may be printed on machine-finish book paper when exceptional results are not needed. The basis weights of the various machine-finish book papers are 60, 70, 80, and 160 pounds.

The sized and supercalendered papers differ from machine finish only in finish. To produce the sized or supercalendered finish, after the paper is dry it is run through a series of stacks or calenders, only the bottom roll being power driven. The paper passes between alternate rolls of compressed paper and chilled iron and is subjected to great pressure. As the paper passes between the rolls, its surface is leveled and polished and made uniform. This kind of paper has a hard finish and may be used as a hard packing. Sized and supercalendered papers print well and will produce good halftone results.

Besides the machine-finish, sized, and supercalendered papers already discussed, various antique stocks are also in common use. Antique papers are distinguished by their rough finish. The basis weights of these are 80, 90, 100, 120, and 140 pounds.

Offset papers also have a somewhat rough finish. The basis weights listed for offset book papers are 80 and 100 pounds.

Coated papers are manufactured in several grades, the cheapest being made to supplement the use of sized and supercalendered papers. The basis weights of coated stock are listed as 100, 120, and 140 pounds. The more expensive coated stock is used for fine illustrated work. In the manufacture of coated stock, machine-finish paper is used and a liquid coating applied by brushing. The sheet is then dried and calendered in the same way as the other book papers. The calender or stack is similar to that used to produce sized and supercalendered paper, except that compressed cotton rollers are employed alternately with chilled iron rollers.

Sulfite writing paper is used extensively throughout the pressroom due to ability to withstand handling. It is of a rough surface but very tough and hard and is used extensively in job and pamphlet work. There are three basis weights: 24, 32, and 40 pounds, figured on a 17-inch by 22-inch sheet.

Bond papers are specially suitable for writing papers, bonds, legal documents, historical papers, etc. The sheet size for basis-weight measurement is 17 by 22 inches. Bond paper is supplied in many finishes and colors. The basis weights of bond papers are listed as 26, 32, and 40 pounds per 1,000 sheets. Bond paper must have a finish suitable for die stamping, steel engraving, and typewriting and writing inks.

Manifold papers are used where multiple copies are needed. The size from which their basis weight is figured is 17 by 22 inches. The basis weights of manifold stock are listed as 14, 16, and 18 pounds per 1,000 sheets. Various finishes and colors are supplied.

In the Government Printing Office, many other **miscellaneous** papers are used, such as ledger, index, mimeograph, ditto, map, postal card, blotting, kraft, wrapping, imitation parchment, etc.

Wood manila is used for **top sheets,** or the outside sheets for packings and tympans. It may be either plain or oiled and is shipped in rolls. In this Office, a special top sheet is used to prevent offset when a job is being run on a perfecting or web press or when being backed up after one side has been printed. This special top sheet carries the trade name Spherekote. The surface of this paper is coated with many minute globules of glass and resembles the screen used for home movie projectors.

Paper has **three outstanding characteristics** with which the pressman should be familiar. All papers have **grain** similar to that in wood. This grain may run either the long way or the short way of the sheet, and the direction of the grain is generally marked on the package in which the paper is delivered. It is very important that the pressman should know the direction of the grain. Papers may be folded much easier with the grain than against it. An otherwise well-printed sheet of paper loses much of its good appearance if it is folded against the grain. A book or sheet of paper will open much easier and stay closed better if the grain runs up and down the pages. If a book or pamphlet is to be wire-stitched, the sheets will not tear away from the stitches readily if the fold is with the grain, which brings the wire against the longer fibers in the paper.

The direction in which the grain in the paper runs may be determined by tearing the paper in both directions. It is decidedly harder to tear against the grain than with it, and the torn portion presents ragged edges. It tears much easier with the grain and leaves a comparatively smooth edge. When sheets are to be printed and used flat, the direction of the grain usually is of little concern. It is not always possible for the pressman to print the stock according to the direction of the grain, as sometimes the paper is delivered to the pressroom already cut in the size to be used and must be printed accordingly.

All paper also has a right and wrong side. In its passage through the papermaking machine one side is uppermost and obtains a better finish. The underside of the paper, which is supported by the wire netting on its passage through the machine, is not so well finished. The underside is known as the **wire side,** and the smooth or upper side the **felt side.** When the sheet of paper is to be printed on only one side, the smooth or felt side should be used. Illustrations should be printed on the felt side whenever possible. Only a brief examination is necessary to determine the difference in the two sides of the paper.

The earliest known **watermark** is dated 1301, and most of the early papermakers used this means to identify their products. Watermarks were used not only as advertisements but also to guarantee the quality of the paper. Early watermarks consisted of symbols, but more elaborate designs have been used, such as illustrations which cover almost the entire sheet.

The same principle is used to produce watermarks in both machine and hand-made papers. The mold or sieve used for hand-made papers is a shallow box of wood, with a fine wire screen stretched across the bottom. The watermark was made by wires bent to form the figure or design. The wires were attached to the upper side of the wire screen, and the sieve was dipped in the vat containing the pulp. As it was lifted, a small layer of fibers remained on the screen, and the water was partially drained from them. Agitation of the mold dispelled most of the remaining water and interwove the fibers to form the sheet of paper. The result was that the paper, over the raised wires which were to form the watermark, was thinner and more transparent than the rest of the paper. The watermark on hand-made papers is on the wire side, although, because of the method used in shaking or agitating the mold, the design of the wire screen is not too noticeable. Laid and wove papers were also produced by hand by the use of raised wires.

Machine-made paper is watermarked by means of a dandy roll. As the web of pulp travels forward on the wire, water drains from it. Before all the water drains away, and just before the pulp passes the last suction box, it moves under the dandy roll. The surface of the dandy roll is traveling at the same speed as the moving web of pulp. The design or watermark is pressed into the pulp with just sufficient force to leave an impression. The watermark design, or wires for laid or wove paper are secured to the dandy roll by soldering, sewing, etc. Unlike hand-made paper, the watermarks of machine-made papers are on the felt or right side of the paper. When it is necessary to print the job on the best side of the paper, it is well to use the watermark as a guide. The watermark can be seen or read properly from the felt side of the sheet. When running rag bond stocks in this Office for use as letterheads or other one-side printing, the head of the eagle in the watermark should point to the viewer's left.

QUESTIONS FOR STUDY AND DISCUSSION

1. What was the earliest known forerunner of paper?
2. What other materials were used before the invention of paper?
3. Where was paper invented?
4. For many centuries who were considered papermakers for the world?
5. In what country was most of the paper made for the early German printers?
6. What machine revolutionized the papermaking industry?
7. Discuss the two general classifications of pulp from which paper is made.
8. Define the meaning of the word "ream." What is meant by substance?
9. What is the cheapest of all printing papers? For what class of printing is it used?
10. Discuss book papers. What is the basis size from which the basis weight is figured for book stock?
11. To what class of printing are coated stocks specially suited?
12. What is the basis size from which the basis weight of bonds is figured?
13. What class of printing is done on bond paper?
14. What special need do manifold papers fill?
15. Discuss the special top sheet used for packing on presses in the Government Printing Office.
16. Why is it important for a pressman to know how to determine the direction of the grain of paper? How may this be determined?
17. What expressions are used to distinguish the right and the wrong side of paper?
18. What is a watermark in paper? How are watermarks made?

CHAPTER 19

Platen Presses

SUBJECT OUTLINE

A. Press mechanism:
1. Pressure.
2. The platen.
3. The bed.
4. The inking mechanism.
5. Flywheel.
6. Trip.
7. Delivery table.
8. Footbrake.
9. Roller frame.
10. Impression lock.
11. Control switch.

B. Operation of platen press:
1. Pack the press.
2. Ink the press.
3. Check height of rollers.
4. Placing chase on bed of press.
5. Placing guides:
   a. Pull impression on top sheet.
   b. Place guides.
6. Position the grippers.
7. The overlay sheet for make-ready.

C. Care of platen presses:
1. Regulating ink flow:
   a. Thumbscrews.
   b. Roller trucks and bed bearers.
2. Washing up.

On platen presses the impression is delivered over the entire surface of the form simultaneously, the flat surface of the form and of the packing or tympan being brought together under great pressure. For each square inch of an ordinary type form to be printed, 75 pounds of pressure is necessary, and solids require even more. When the number of square inches in a form is multiplied by at least 75 pounds, it may be seen readily that the press must be constructed solidly to withstand such pressure.

The bed and platen can be made heavy and rigid enough to handle any form, but the extra weight slows down the operating speed of the press.

Since platens are now used to print only the lighter forms, the more cumbersome construction is seldom used. The platen and press bed are heavily ribbed to provide the rigidity required. Since there is some give or elasticity to iron, this causes bearing off or weak impression in the center of the platen. Makeready counteracts this.

Some press manufacturers make the surface of the platen slightly convex, that is, slightly higher in the center than at the edges, to overcome this undesirable feature of the platen press.

When the platen is to be adjusted, five letters, each of which measures 72 points or one square inch, are locked within the press chase. The letters best suited for this purpose are M's or W's. They are measured with a type-high gage to assure that they are the correct height and locked one at each of the four corners within the chase, one-half inch from the chase edge. The fifth letter is locked directly in the center of the chase. The packing used at this time should consist of about three manila sheets and one pressboard.

It will be noticed that the underside of the platen has four or five impression screws locked into position by jamnuts or locknuts. A sheet is pulled on light coated paper and the impression on the back noted. The press does not need to be inked to do this as all adjustments are made from impression only. The platen is then adjusted by raising or lowering the impression screws until an even impression is obtained on the four corner figures. The center figure will probably show a slightly heavier impression.

On presses which use five impression screws, the center screw should be moved from contact with the platen before any of the corners of the platen are adjusted. After the edges of the platen have been adjusted, the center screw is run up until it just touches the underside of the platen. If the center screw is so adjusted that too much pressure is applied, there is danger of cracking the metal platen. After the impression screws have been adjusted, the jamnuts are tightened.

Attached to the lower part of the platen by hinges are two metal grippers which are sometimes equipped with sliding metal fingers to hold the sheet to the tympan. These grippers must clear the printed form. Sometimes it is necessary to rig a frisket between the two grippers so that the printed sheet will not stick to the form. The frisket may be either a string or a cutout of manila paper.

The bed of the press is a flat surface which accommodates the form and chase. When the chase is put to the bed of the press, it is held in position by two lugs on the bottom of the bed which fit into grooves at the foot of the chase, and at the top by a clamp which is hinged to the top of the bed, holding the chase by spring tension. On each side of the bed are two bearers on which the roller trucks ride. These bearers should be kept clean and free from oil. The beds of earlier platen presses are constructed solidly and no adjustment may be made.

The ink plate, in the shape of a disk, distributes the ink to the form rollers. Above this disk is the ink fountain from which the ink flow is regulated by means of a ratchet. The form rollers are carried by the roller carriage and they ink the form twice for each impression.

The rollers are composition, and on each end of the roller is a circular fiber or expandable roller truck. These roller trucks ride on the bed bearers as the rollers ink the form. When the roller carriage is at its topmost position, the roller nearest the fountain touches the fountain roller and ink is distributed first to the top roller and then to the ink disk from the roller.

Because of the conformation of platen presses, the form rollers almost exhaust their supply of ink on the downward movement when inking heavy forms. Then, on the upward stroke, the rollers pass over the form in the same relative position, and the solids within the form are not properly inked. Several devices have been employed to overcome this fault. Oscillating distributor rollers similar to the vibrator rollers on cylinder presses may be placed in the roller carriage. This assures better ink distribution, since these rollers replace the ink removed from the form rollers on their first passage over the form. The use of large and small form rollers insures that the smaller rollers will not pass over the form on the upward stroke in the same position as the larger rollers.

A patented device is also used which prevents the lowest roller from touching the form on the downward stroke, but releases it at the extreme lower motion of the carriage so that it will distribute a fresh supply of ink on its upward stroke. It is best, however, to print only light forms on the platen presses, and those containing solids should be assigned to the cylinder machines.

The flywheel is a large wheel, usually mounted on the left side of the press, which provides momentum and facilitates smooth operation of the press. The trip is a hand lever also located at the left side of the press, just inside the flywheel. When the trip is thrown forward or away from the feeder, the press will run, but the form and tympan will not come in contact with each other. The feed table is located in a convenient position to the right of the feeder and is adjustable. The delivery table is placed directly in front of the feeder just to the rear of the platen, and the sheets are placed on this level surface after they are printed.

A footbrake is provided to stop the press after the power has been shut off.

A roller frame composed of two heavily constructed arms, one on each side of the machine, conveys the roller carriage. The roller frame is so pivoted as to give proper roller motion while the press is running, the rollers being on the ink disk while the impression is being made, and on and below the form while the press is in its open position.

The platen and press bed are brought together on impression by means of the cam gear and the pinion gear which is on the main drive shaft. An impression lock used on platen presses moves into place to hold the platen steady. This lock is located just below the delivery board of the press. The electric control switch is usually located at the front of the press on the left side. To pack the platen a piece of pressboard, four sheets of sized and supercalendered stock, and an oiled manila top sheet will be needed. The less packing used, the less danger there will be of wrinkles and lumps. All the sheets, with the exception of the pressboard, should be wide enough to reach under both tympan bails and about 4 inches longer than the sheet to be printed. All four corners of the white and oiled manila sheets may be trimmed at an angle of 45 degrees. However, the packing must be large enough to accommodate the entire form.

A lip of about one-half inch is folded to the edge of each sheet to go under the bottom bail. The creased edges of all the sheets so folded are then placed together evenly with the manila sheet on top, the crease placed along the lower edge of the platen, the sheets held firmly, and the lower bail clamped into place. The pressboard is then placed under the bottom white sheet, the packing smoothed, the tail of the sheets pulled tight, and the upper bail clamped in place.

Any excess paper on the tail end of the packing is torn off. If there are any wrinkles in the packing, the clamps should be loosened and the wrinkles smoothed out. The press should not be left unattended when the clamps are in the open position, as serious damage will result if the press is run while they are open.

To ink up the press, place the rollers in their lowest position and wipe the disk plate with a clean rag to remove all dust and lint. The flywheel is turned by hand until the rollers come into a position where they can be wiped. Throughout most of the makeready operation the press is run by turning the flywheel by hand. Most platen presses operate by turning the flywheel away from the feeder, but in some cases it turns in the opposite direction.

A small amount of ink may now be applied to the left side of the disk. The dried part of the ink in the can should be removed, and the surface scraped lightly until the required amount of ink has been obtained. Less ink is needed for makeready than when the job is being run. It is best to ink up the press before the form has been placed in the bed, as this allows better ink distribution and prevents the form being clogged by lumps of ink.

The height of the rollers should be checked before the form is placed on the bed. A type-high roller gage may be used to check the height of the rollers above the surface of the bed. If any changes are required, either larger or smaller roller trucks must be used on the ends of the roller stocks or the bearers or trucks built up. If expandable roller trucks are to be used, adjustments of rollers can be made by gaging height, then use an adjustment wrench to raise or lower the rollers as may be required by different jobs.

Before the form is placed in the bed, the back is cleaned and the form carded and planed down on the imposing stone. With the press rollers in their lowest position, the surface of the bed is wiped with a clean rag. Now the chase may be placed on the bed of the press, taking care to avoid hitting the surface of the type on any part of the press or damaging the rollers with the edge of the chase. The chase must be held in the proper position with the quoins up and to the right and the grooves for the lugs to the bottom. It is then placed gently on the bed from the right side of the press, so that the lugs at the bottom of the bed fit into the grooves in the chase.

The form is held with the left hand, the chase clamp raised with the right, the chase pushed flat against the bed, the clamp released, and the chase tapped lightly on its upper edge with a hammer or wrench to position it properly.

The press should be run by hand until it is almost on impression, and the form sighted to be sure that the grippers clear all printing portions of the type. Now an impression may be pulled on the top sheet, but keep in mind that it is always best to start with a light impression to avoid damage to the form.

Determine the correct margins and mark the bottom and side guide-lines on the tympan accordingly. It is on these lines that the bottom and side guides will be placed. The impression is then wiped from the top sheet with a rag and Varsol.

The bottom guides should be placed about one-sixth of the way in from each end, and the side guide about 2 inches from the lower edge of the sheet. These patent guides are pinned through the manila top sheet only. An impression is now pulled with the sheet positioned to the guides; and after the position has been OK'd, the guides are tapped into place lightly with a wrench or small hammer. The small points in the face of the guides engage the drawsheet and prevent the guides from slipping. Sealing wax may also be used for a long run or when a heavy sheet is being printed.

A printed sheet is then placed to the guides and the grippers positioned. Whenever the grippers are moved, a wrench which fits the gripper nuts exactly should be used to avoid rounding them. The right gripper may be moved within 1 pica of the printed form, but the left gripper must be placed so as to clear both the print and the guide tongue. When this is not possible, a frisket of paper or cards must be used to extend between the two grippers and hold the sheet firmly to the tympan.

To pull a sheet for overlay, a sheet of the stock on which the job is to be printed is placed to the guides, a sheet of sized and supercalendered paper of the same size placed over it, and an impression pulled.

It should not be necessary at this time to add to or subtract from the packing, as the proper impression should have been determined when the OK or revise sheet was pulled.

The overlay sheet is prepared in the manner described in the preceding chapter, the only exception being that, in making ready for the platen press, slightly more impression is required. Therefore, the limitation of only three spots in any one position does not apply, since some pages may require four or even five sheets of tissue or folio to bring up the low places. After the sheet is carefully marked and spotted up it may be hung in the tympan. Unlike makeready for the cylinder press, the platen makeready may be stabbed after spotting up.

To hang the overlay sheet, the upper bail is loosened, the manila sheet and two white sheets raised, and the spot sheet matched to the stab marks and pasted to one of the white sheets in the packing. The pressboard is removed from the bottom of the packing and placed just over the spot sheet, the packing smoothed to prevent wrinkles, and the upper foil clamped on the sheets.

Some forms may require two spot sheets, but generally any further spots may be applied to the face of the spot sheet already in the packing. As in all printing, the ink chosen should suit the stock and the nature of work being printed.

On a job of any length the ink fountain must be used. It is usually filled about half full or just sufficient to finish the job. Flow of ink from the fountain is regulated by adjusting thumbscrews, or flow screws, starting with the center screw and working equally to both ends of the fountain. The flow should be adjusted to the job being printed, as heavy areas require more ink and lighter areas less. Care should be taken to prevent setting screws too tightly as it may cause serious damage to the fountain.

The roller trucks and bed bearers should be wiped carefully with a rag and Varsol. These trucks and bearers should be watched carefully during the run to see that they do not accumulate a coating of ink, oil, or other foreign matter. Clean trucks and bearers insure the proper turning of the form rollers on the form and prevent damage to the rollers.

Varsol is generally used for the press washup. The rollers are run to a position off the ink disk by turning the flywheel by hand, and the disk is cleaned. The flywheel should be turned by hand until the top roller is about one-fourth of an inch away from the disk, and the rollers washed.

The remaining rollers are then moved up and cleaned in the same position.

Certain safety factors must be considered in the operation of any kind of machinery. Regardless of the safety features incorporated in the design of platen presses, accidents can happen. The apprentice should give his undivided attention to the operation of the press. He should not reach into moving machinery to retrieve sheets or rags, to apply ink, or to make any press adjustments. Although damaged machinery may be repaired or replaced, personal injury may have lasting results.

QUESTIONS FOR STUDY AND DISCUSSION

1. How much pressure is required for each square inch to be printed?
2. Describe the platen of the press.
3. Discuss the process of adjusting the platen.
4. What is the function of the metal grippers which are attached to the lower part of the platen?
5. By what means is a chase held in position in the bed of a press?
6. Describe the inking mechanism of platen presses.
7. What purpose does the flywheel serve? The trip? The delivery table? The footbrake?
8. For what kinds of printing are platen presses specially suitable?
9. Describe the process of packing the platen.
10. Discuss the operation of inking the press.
11. How may the height of rollers be checked?
12. When a chase is to be placed on the bed of the press, what precautions should be taken?
13. What preparations are made before an impression is pulled?
14. What precautions should be observed when the grippers are being placed in position?
15. Describe the process of pulling a sheet for overlay, preparing it for makeready, and hanging it in the platen press.
16. By what means are the guides anchored to the top sheet of the packing?
17. How is the flow of ink from the fountain regulated?
18. Discuss the washup for the platen press.

CHAPTER 20

Packing Vertical Presses

SUBJECT OUTLINE

A. Review press controls.
B. Prepare the press.
C. Remove feedboard.
D. Remove old packing.
E. Apply new packing:
    1. Permanent.

2. Temporary:
    a. Medium.
    b. Hard.
    c. Soft.
F. Observe safety precautions.

The preceding chapter dealt with packing platen presses, and this chapter concerns packing vertical presses. On platen machines the impression is applied simultaneously to the whole surface of the sheet and form, whereas on cylinder presses the impression is applied to the paper in only a very narrow strip at a time, as the cylinder turns. The form may be the same as that used on the platen press, but the packing and the sheet to be printed are held to a cylinder which revolves over the form. This cylinder is geared directly to the bed of the press, to keep uniform speed during printing. The sheet to be printed is held to the cylinder and the packing by means of mechanical grippers.

This principle applies to all cylinder presses, but the vertical differs in one important respect. The bed of most cylinder presses is horizontal and the cylinder revolves above it in fixed bearings; on the vertical press, both bed and cylinder move in opposition to each other with a vertical motion. While the other presses may be hand-fed, this is impossible on the vertical, as it is strictly an automatic machine.

The vertical press is a relatively new machine, both in engineering and design, as most of the earlier presses were of the horizontal or platen type. Some of the earliest verticals were sent to European countries for demonstration purposes. An indication of their popularity is the fact that during the first 15 years of their manufacture, more than 10,000 vertical presses were sold. They were manufactured to take the place of the old-style platen job presses and the small and slower flatbed cylinder machines which were used for job printing.

Vertical presses are compact in construction and require only 4 by 5 feet of floorspace. They are simple to operate, all adjustments can be easily and quickly made, and the safety features incorporated are many and accurate. Press speeds on the earlier models were from 2,000 to 3,600 impressions per hour; but later models range from 3,000 to 5,000. Unlike platen presses, the vertical machines handle all kinds of job-work, maintain accurate register, and also produce good halftone and process colorwork.

Press controls should be **reviewed** before the process of packing the press is discussed. Before the machine is started, it should be clear of all foreign material which might cause damage. When the power is turned on, the pump and drive pulley are set in motion. To start the press, the belt-tightening lever is pulled toward the rear of the machine; to stop it, this same lever is pushed to the forwardmost position.

To **prepare the press**, the first step is to have clear working space available to either the press bed or press cylinder. The feeder mechanism should be swung out of running position, and the machine run until the cylinder is at its lowest point of travel. Then the feeder lock, which is located on the flywheel side of the press and just back of the flywheel, is unlocked and the feeder moved out of position. The press can be run while the feeder is out of position without damage to any of the machinery. It can be run until the cylinder is at its topmost stroke and the delivery fingers have just started to move away from the grippers.

A key at the left side of the feeding table holds the table in place. This key is moved to the left until disengaged, and the left side of the feeder table is raised to an angle of about 45 degrees. From this position the **feedboard may be removed** from the press. On the upper part of the press frame are two triangular metal holders which retain the feeder table while it is not in use.

Now the **old packing can be removed**. The cylinder may be turned to any desired position by using a pin wrench which fits the holes just inside the cylinder bearers. The cylinder should be turned toward the press bed, which is the direction in which it turns while printing. A considerable amount of pressure must be exerted to start the cylinder turning, as the stop cam lever on the right end of the cylinder must be disengaged from the cylinder stop cam. This lever and cam should always be engaged before the press is started, otherwise serious damage will result. On later models, a pin on the left side of the cylinder must be disengaged before the cylinder can be rotated by hand, and reengaged before the press is run under power.

The cylinder is turned until the packing reel on the tail end of the top sheet comes into view. The pin wrench is placed in the holes on the left end of this reel to disengage the ratchet which holds the reel in position. Then the tail of the packing may be disengaged and the cylinder turned forward until the gripper bar comes into view. This bar, which also acts as a packing clamp, is held in position by three screws which clamp it in place. Either a small pin wrench or nail set is used to loosen these screws until the gripper bar is released. The gripper bar is now removed from the cylinder, and placed gently on the feeder to avoid damaging it, and the old packing removed. The metal cylinder surface should then be cleaned and oiled.

In the application of **new packing** on vertical presses, both permanent and temporary must be used. The **permanent** packing usually consists of three sheets of manila stock 0.006 of an inch thick.

The **temporary** packing is composed of six sheets of sized and supercalendered stock 0.003 of an inch thick, and one manila top sheet 0.006 of an inch thick. The three manila sheets should be wide enough to cover the entire surface of the cylinder from bearer to bearer, and long enough to allow about 1 inch to fold under the gripper bar. The six sheets of sized and supercalendered paper should be the same size as the manila, and the manila top drawsheet is cut to 20 by 21 inches. The 21-inch length allows 1 inch to fold over the gripper edge with a sharp crease and enough extra to fasten on the reel at the tail end of the sheet.

On normal jobs, it is recommended that two loose sheets about 0.004 of an inch thick, size 12½ by 19 inches, be placed loosely in the packing and later removed for makeready purposes. The total thickness of the entire packing is now 0.05 of an inch thick. Since the cylinder on vertical presses is undercut 0.05 of an inch to insure satisfactory printing, the thickness of the packing and the sheet to be printed must total at least this amount.

The manila sheets are folded separately, but all the white sheets may be folded at the same time. The manila sheets are hung one at a time on the cylinder, where the gripper bar clamps the packing. The packing pins are pressed through the sheets by starting from the center of the cylinder and working toward both ends until all pins are pressed through the fold. All the white sheets may be hung on at the same time, and the pins pressed through them, as was done with the manila sheets. After the white sheets are placed on the cylinder, the manila top sheet is put in position, and the gripper bar replaced. This bar will fit on the cylinder in only one position. The three screws which hold the gripper bar to the cylinder are then tightened.

The cylinder is moved forward with the pin wrench until the reel rod comes into position, the packing being smoothed out at the same time. The outside edges of the top sheet are now angled off from the end of the cylinder surface to form the tail, which is slipped under the reel rod. The tail of the top sheet is pulled taut, creased along one edge of the square reel rod, and backed off the reel rod until the sheet folds over on itself.

The reel rod is then turned forward as far as possible with the hand, the pin wrench engaged in the rod, and the ratchet fastened. The packing of the vertical cylinder is then completed. The cylinder is turned forward with the pin wrench, and the packing is inspected to see that it lies perfectly smooth and without wrinkles on the cylinder. The cylinder must be turned forward until the stop cam lever snaps into place. This safety feature must never be neglected.

The **permanent packing** may remain on the cylinder for some time without being changed, but the temporary packing should be changed for every job requiring makeready. The composition of the **temporary packing** may be varied to suit the particular job being printed. A temporary packing, such as the one previously described, would produce a **medium** or average packing. Two top sheets could be used with fewer sheets of sized and supercalendered paper to furnish a hard packing. In a soft packing the sized and supercalendered filler sheets would be replaced by machine finish or newsprint paper.

Let us now consider some of the safety precautions which are to be observed while packing vertical presses. The power supply should be shut off from the switch mounted on the press, since use of the stop button alone is not sufficient. Avoid hitting the knuckles of the hand when turning the cylinder or using a pen wrench. Although it takes a little effort to remove the cylinder from the cam lock, the cylinder moves freely after this lock has been disengaged. The cylinder should always be turned forward or toward the press bed when moving. The cylinder cam lock and lever should be engaged before running the machine or before leaving it for any length of time. The feedboard lock should always be kept in good operating condition, as it should work freely enough to be manipulated by hand. If this lock shows any tendency to bind, a small amount of oil may be applied to the slide, or the lock may be filed down until it works properly. The gripper bar must be handled with care to avoid damage to the bar or injury to the hands.

QUESTIONS FOR STUDY AND DISCUSSION

1. How does the application of the impression differ in platen presses and vertical presses?

2. In what important respect does the operation of the vertical differ from that of other cylinder presses?

3. What is done to prepare the press before removing the old packing?

4. Describe the process of removing old packing.

5. Discuss two kinds of packing that may be used on vertical presses.

6. What safety precautions should be observed in packing cylinder presses?

CHAPTER 21

Packing Cylinder Presses

SUBJECT OUTLINE

A. Removing old packings.
B. Cleaning cylinder.
C. Preparing new packings:
    1. Permanent.
    2. Temporary.
    3. Thickness of packings.
    4. Composition of packings.

    5. Arrangement of sheets.
    6. Preparation of sheets.
D. Hanging new packings:
    1. Permanent.
    2. Temporary.
    3. Drawsheet.

A well-prepared packing is the foundation for a good makeready and a satisfactorily printed job. It is possible to apply a packing so that there will be no trouble from that source from start to finish of the press run, no matter how long the run may be.

In the work of packing the cylinder, the first step is to **remove the old packings.** All small pieces of paper which may have stuck under the clamps are removed. The next step is to **clean the metal surface of the cylinder.** All dirt or rust is removed by using a clean rag and Varsol, and a thin coat of machine oil is applied to the packing bearing surface. Any nicks or burrs on the metal cylinder surface caused by stabbing the packing too deeply should be removed with fine emery cloth.

When the cylinder is ready, the **new packings** may be **prepared.** Two kinds of packing are used for cylinder presses, **permanent** packing which may remain on the press for many jobs without being changed, and **temporary** packing which is changed for each job requiring makeready. Both packings are held to the front of the cylinder by a series of pins about one-eighth of an inch thick and about one-half inch long, which are spaced across the cylinder about 4 inches apart. The packing is placed on these pins and is held securely in place by means of the packing clamps, which hold the packing securely on the pins by means of tension. The protruding ends of the pins extend through holes in the clamps on some presses.

The back or tail end of the top sheet of each packing is held by a reel. One reel holds the top sheet of the permanent packing, and another reel holds the top sheet of the temporary packing. These reels consist of steel rods about seven-eighths of an inch square, which run the width of the cylinder. The tail end of the top sheet is wound on the reel and pulled tight by use of the pin wrench. The reel is then held in place by means of a ratchet on its end and a dog on the cylinder.

The question that arises at this point is, How many sheets are needed to make the correct thickness of the packings? To answer this, the height of the cylinder bearer and the amount of packing required to bring the top sheet of the packing level with the cylinder bearers must be known. A list of the various bed and cylinder bearer heights for all presses now in general use is given herewith.

Bed bearer heights:	*Inch*
Miehle presses except 29, 41, and 46	0.9167
Miehle 29, 41, and 46	.914
Miehle two-color	.914
Miller presses	.916
Cylinder undercut (cylinder bearers):	
Miehle vertical	.050
Miehle 29	.060
Miehle bobtail	.109
Miehle two-color	.064
First cylinder Miehle Perfector	.070
Second cylinder Miehle Perfector	.078
All other Miehle cylinder presses	.070
Miller Simplex and SY presses	.054
Miehle sheet-fed rotary presses, impression cylinder	.050
Plate cylinder	1.89

Let us assume that a packing is to be applied to a cylinder press. The indicated undercut is 0.070 of an inch. The total thickness of the permanent packing, the temporary packing, and the sheet being printed must be at least this amount.

If the sheet to be printed is 0.003 of an inch thick, this amount is deducted from 0.070, which leaves 0.067 of an inch. To this should be added 0.002 of an inch for impression squeeze, giving a total of 0.069 of an inch as the correct thickness of the packing. This amount of impression squeeze (0.002) is not sufficient for most forms, but will provide a safe starting point for makeready.

What, then, is the composition of the packings? It may be worked out in this manner: nine sheets of manila, 0.006 of an inch thick; five white hanger sheets of sized and supercalendered paper, 0.003 of an inch thick; and one sheet of the stock to be printed, 0.003 of an inch. This gives a total for the temporary and permanent packing and the sheet of stock to be printed of 0.072 of an inch, which is just the amount needed.

How should these **sheets be arranged** in the packing? A long run will require careful makeready on a hard packing. Seven sheets of manila will be needed for the permanent packing and five white sheets with two manila sheets over them for the temporary packing.

The next step is the **preparation of the sheets.** The manila sheets should be cleanly cut at the edges and squared by the cutter and should be long enough to cover the packing surface of the cylinder, with about 2 inches left over for the folded lip. They should be wide enough to cover the width of the cylinder, with about 1 inch to spare from the bearers on each side. Two of the manila sheets (one top sheet each for the temporary and permanent packing) must be about 15 inches longer than the others to allow them to be reeled in as top sheets. The white hanger sheets should be larger than the sheets to be printed, after allowance is made for the lip. For the permanent packing, all manila sheets must be pasted together on the lip, and the lip of the bottom manila sheet glued to the cylinder under the packing clamps. It is best to use a good grade of iron glue or animal glue to secure the paper to the metal cylinder.

To suit the job to be run, the sheet which comprises the temporary packing may be changed or rearranged to obtain the desired packing, hard, soft, or medium. On some jobs which require careful makeready or close register, or on forms which contain illustrations, it is advisable to paste the lip edge of the sheets in the temporary packing together and also to paste the bottom sheet of this packing to the top sheet of the permanent packing.

A very important process in making a satisfactory packing is the folding of the lip. A smooth table large enough to accommodate the packing sheets is necessary. For the manila sheets, each lip is folded separately. Various methods are used by pressmen, one of which may be described as follows: The manila sheet is laid on the table with the ends to be lipped or folded nearest the pressman. The sheet is folded over, with about 2 inches allowed for the lip and with the two edges of the sheet perfectly even at the start of the fold. Then the sheet is folded lightly to determine if the 2-inch width is carried evenly across. It may be necessary to change the fold slightly to ensure this. After the fold is accurate, press it firmly.

The sheet should then be turned over and away from the pressman for about a foot and a half of its length and refolded hard on this side. This ensures an absolutely straight fold which will lie at on the cylinder clamp edge and give no trouble. The remaining manila sheets in the permanent packing should be folded in the same manner. This includes the six short manila sheets and the long one, which is the reel sheet. The lips of the filler sheets used in the temporary packing may be folded together, but the manila sheets for this packing should be folded separately.

To **hang the new packings**, they must be applied to the cylinder separately and the top sheet drawn tight. The **permanent packing** is applied by gluing the lip of the bottom manila sheet to the clamp edge of the cylinder without allowing glue to get on the packing bearing surface. Just enough should be used to make certain that the packing is held snugly. After the glue is applied, the first of the manila sheets is placed so that the lip edge is even with the clamp edge of the cylinder. Fold the lip edge straight across the cylinder by using the thumb and forefinger of each hand, starting at the middle and working evenly to each end of the cylinder. Then the sheet is centered with equal margins from each cylinder bearer, folded, and placed on the packing pins, starting in the center and working evenly to both ends.

The remaining short manila sheets of the permanent packing are put on in a similar manner, each being glued carefully to keep the glue on the clamp edge of the sheet. The longer manila sheet will be the top sheet of the permanent packing. After this sheet is glued in place, the cylinder clamp is closed in the following manner: The pin wrench is put in place in a cylinder clamp, forced down toward the center of the cylinder until the clamp holder passes the lug which holds it, and then slid slightly toward the middle of the cylinder, where it remains in place. Then the shooflies are lowered gently to the packing, and the cylinder is run around to fasten the top sheet on the tail end.

The control is operated with the left hand when the press is run around to smooth the sheets on the cylinder. The right hand is carefully and snugly held on the packing to smooth it while the press is in motion. The press is run around until the reel is in position to receive the tail end of the top sheet of the permanent packing, which is placed under the permanent packing reel, the reel nearest the front of the press. The tail end of this sheet is then pulled snugly in place to make sure that the packing is straight, even, and free from wrinkles, and held by both hands firmly against one side of the square of the packing reel, while the reel is backed off slightly. The sheet is then folded so that when the reel is taken up, the sheet firmly binds against itself and will not slip. The pin wrench is inserted in the near end of the reel and the packing pulled snug. If too much pressure is applied, there is danger of breaking the top sheet or pulling it from the clamps. The dog on the cylinder is now put in place on the ratchet, the pin wrench removed, and the excess end of the tail sheet torn off.

After the permanent packing has been hung in place, the temporary packing may be applied. The press is run to a position where the grippers open while on the top position of the cylinder. The shooflies are carefully raised, the packing clamps again opened, and the forward edge of the permanent packing inspected for wrinkles or lumps. If the packing has been correctly applied, no trouble should be experienced. For long runs, all sheets of the temporary packing are glued together and the bottom sheet is glued to the lip edge of the top sheet of the permanent packing. On short runs this is not always necessary. The lips on the white sheets of the temporary packing are folded as previously described, except that the four sheets may be folded at the same time and glued together, before they are placed on the cylinder. Glue or paste should be used only on the lip of the packing. The white sheets are placed on the cylinder in the same manner and positioned so that they will cover the form to be printed.

Next, the short manila sheet is folded, glued, and put in place; and the manila top sheet of the temporary packing is glued in the same manner. The packing clamps are then locked, the shooflies closed gently, and the press run around until the reel for the temporary packing comes into position.

Often the back end of the bottom white sheet in the temporary packing is also glued in place to make a drawsheet or solid foundation to which the makeready may be attached. The tail end of the temporary packing top sheet is now reeled in, in the manner already described. The press is securely packed and ready for the makeready. A good packing is essential to a good makeready, and a straight fold is essential to a good packing.

QUESTIONS FOR STUDY AND DISCUSSION

1. What is the first step in repacking cylinder presses?
2. How may the metal surface of the cylinder be cleaned?
3. Name the two kinds of packing used on cylinder presses.
4. What factors must be known before the thickness needed for the packing can be figured?
5. Discuss the kinds of paper needed to make temporary and permanent packings.
6. How are these sheets arranged in the packing?
7. What preparation of the sheets is necessary?
8. Describe the process of hanging the permanent packing.
9. How is the temporary packing applied?
10. What is the purpose of the drawsheets?

CHAPTER 22

Why Is Makeready Necessary?

SUBJECT OUTLINE

A. Theory of letterpress printing.
B. Four main factors which necessitate regulation of pressure:
1. Paper surfaces.
2. Nature of the job.
3. Form from which print is to be made.

4. Necessity to compensate for compression:
   a. Stresses on printing units.
   b. Form materials.
   c. Packings.
C. Printing without makeready:
   1. Newspaper presses.
   2. Multicolor presses.
   3. Aniline printing.

For many years press manufacturers, pressmen, and plate, type, paper, and ink makers have been striving to eliminate the necessity for makeready. So far their efforts have been successful for certain grades of printing but not encouraging for others.

The theory of letterpress printing is that if a smooth, ink-receptive sheet of paper and a level plate of type form are brought together at the proper place or speed, with the correct kind of ink, a satisfactory print will be obtained. The pressman and the makers of the supplies used by him are striving toward this end. However, the materials used by pressmen vary to such a great degree that makeready is necessary on all but the cheapest grades of work.

The pressman resorts to makeready not because he likes the extra work it entails, but because it is the only possible means of obtaining a passable print which will remain that way throughout the press run. Many shops have rules to eliminate makeready, such as required packing thicknesses, amount of underlay, etc. Frequently these rules are slighted by the workers in order to produce acceptable printing and to retain their positions. Yet such shops still maintain that makeready has been eliminated.

131

Four main factors necessitate the regulation of the pressure in the packing thickness or form height for printing. First, paper surfaces, as different stocks require various amounts of pressure to print the same form; second, the nature of the job, as each job is made to order and uses a different form; third, the form to be printed, since it may be composed of any of the materials from which prints can be made; fourth, the necessity to compensate for compression and stretch, since these strains affect the press parts, packing, form, and the sheet being printed. These are the four main factors which necessitate makeready.

Anyone familiar with presswork knows that different paper surfaces require various amounts of pressure to be printed. Forms which could be printed without trouble on soft, absorbent papers without makeready require a great deal of pressure regulation to print properly on bond, coated, or other nonabsorbent surfaces. In recent years many new surfaces have been found to be printable by improvements in inks and the development of special printing machines.

As an example, a solid plate which is perfectly level and type high can be placed on a press which is in perfect operating condition. The packing is then adjusted to supply the correct pressure for printing the cut on calendered paper when using a suitable ink. With this arrangement a satisfactory print can be made without makeready. The print obtained will not be of the best quality, but it will be passable for a limited number of impressions. The cut must be given enough pressure from a flat packing to print the center solid portion. When this is done, the edges of the plate will print too heavily and be indented in the stock. For best printing, the edges should be printed with several thousandths of an inch less pressure than the center. If the job is allowed to run for a number of impressions and without this adjustment, the edges would become worn and the cut would no longer be usable.

If an attempt is made to print this cut on other papers such as enamel, bond, manifold, or embossed stocks under the same form and packing conditions, even though an ink suited to the stock being printed is used, the results will be unsatisfactory. The printing pressure necessary to get even a poor print would have to be increased by 0.010 of an inch or more. This added pressure would cause incorrect surface travel and make it necessary to increase the form height. On some stocks, a passable print could not be obtained unless the center of the cut is given more pressure than the edges by overlaying or interlaying. This example should show it is not possible to print the more difficult printing surfaces without makeready.

Even though additional pressure would produce a fair print of the cut on any stock, how would this affect the normal form? Most forms are composed of both light and solid areas. Anyone who has tried to print a letterpress form knows that the light form areas, isolated lines of type, or rules, require much less pressure to print than the more solid parts of the form. If additional pressure is provided to the entire form, the light areas punch through the sheet and into the packing. The fact that different form areas and various paper surfaces require unequal amounts of pressure is one of the main reasons for makeready.

The second factor is the **nature of the job** itself. In modern printing, the material to be printed may be only 0.001 of an inch thick, it may be cardboard, or even wood, and the surface to be printed may range from spongy softness to glasslike hardness. The amount of material to be printed may be only several pieces or several million. The size of each print may range from postage-stamp size to a large section of a billboard. The form may be composed of extremely large solids or of fine lines or dots hardly visible to the naked eye. Therefore, because the jobs are not at all standardized, makeready is necessary to produce the best possible print for each job.

The **form from which the print is made** may be foundry type, linotype, or monotype; metal plates, electrotypes, stereotypes, or originals; or other plates such as plastic, rubber, wood, linoleum, etc. When plates are used, they may be mounted either on blocks of metal or wood or may be patent-base mounted. The entire form may be composed of one or several of these materials, and makeready is much easier and more economical than to try to bring all form areas to equal height. All form materials are made as nearly type high as mechanically possible; however, certain materials vary in height between the time they are produced and the time they are delivered to the pressman.

The final reason for makeready is the **necessity to compensate for compression** and stretch. The two parts of the printing unit, the bed and impression surface, are forced apart when the necessary pressure for printing is delivered. This press give is very noticeable on platen presses; it varies on flatbed machines with the construction of the press; and on rotary presses is hardly an important factor. The wide range of **stresses** on the different types of **printing** units are caused by the method in which the impression is delivered.

Form materials are also compressed various degrees under pressure, as different kinds of metal compress differently. Wood bases are very susceptible to printing strains, while patent bases are hardly affected.

Fortunately for the pressman, the wood base has been eliminated for most jobs.

Packings give under the pressure of printing, depending on the hardness of the materials used in the packing. Likewise, the material being printed is subject to pressure. The only way in which compression of the press parts and printing materials can be compensated is by makeready.

Great strides have been made toward the elimination of makeready, but it is not an immediate possibility for all kinds of letterpress printing. Today the amount of work produced without makeready of any kind is limited and is accomplished by the use of special packings or prepared plates. The amount of makeready which has been saved by improving printing materials has greatly speeded up presswork and eliminated a great percentage of the pressman's troubles. For the good of all concerned with letterpress printing, these improvements must continue.

However, some jobs can be printed without makeready, some can sometimes be printed without makeready, and for some, makeready is absolutely essential to obtain a satisfactory print.

The largest percentage of **printing without makeready** is accomplished on rotary presses. Makeready is not necessary on many of these machines because of the kind of printing generally done on them for which they are specially made. Newspapers, weekly or monthly magazines, aniline printing on nonporous stocks, and cheaper grades of books are printed on rotary presses with little or no makeready.

Newspaper presses use a soft packing on the impression cylinders, and the print is made on soft absorbent paper with suitable ink. For this kind of printing, quantity is more important than quality. To print illustrations on newsprint, a coarse halftone screen which is visible to the naked eye must be used, and excessive impression or poor ink coverage is not too objectionable.

On newspaper presses the run is usually made or started without makeready. However, if insufficient pressure for printing is found on some plate or area, the pressure is increased by underlaying or interlaying until a satisfactory print is obtained.

The less costly magazines are printed in color on specially made presses. These machines which are known as **multicolor presses** have four or five plate cylinders which print the web of paper in different colors on one impression cylinder. The impression cylinder is packed with a hard packing to produce sharp, clear impressions. The paper used for the printing of magazines is of fair quality and allows the printing of finer screen halftones than can be used for newspapers. Other kinds of work printed on multicolor presses are labels and catalogs on calendered or coated papers. The runs on these machines are usually long, ranging from 100,000 to 1,000,000 or more copies. Bear in mind that, even though the stocks on which this kind of work is printed are hard surfaced, the base of the paper is fairly soft as compared with some stocks used for printing.

The method of printing on multicolor presses where four or more plates strike in the same place on a single impression cylinder makes the general use of overlay impossible. If each plate cylinder requires additional pressure in the same area of the impression cylinder, a spot of makeready can be placed in the packing for this area.

Printing on multicolor presses is generally considered to be accomplished without makeready, but this is hardly true. Most of the large shops use plates for printing illustrations which are specially treated before being sent to the press. As more solid areas of plates will require more impression, the plates are graduated in thickness. The most solid areas are the most thick, the middle tones of the halftone slightly thinner, and the highlights or smallest dots in the plate are made thinner still. By making the plate in this manner, much of the operation of regulating the pressure for printing has been eliminated. Actually the need for makeready still exists, but it has been partially remedied.

In multicolor shops where prepared plates are not used, the makeready must be completed by the pressman under the plates in order to obtain a satisfactory print which would not cause excessive plate wear during the run.

Another kind of printing which is handled without makeready is **aniline printing**. Surfaces such as wax paper, glassine, cellophane, kraft paper, etc., are printed on a press designed especially for this kind of printing. Rubber plates are used and inks which dry by vaporization. On such machines the ink is transferred to the paper by the elasticity of the plates rather than of the stock or of the impression cylinder.

QUESTIONS FOR STUDY AND DISCUSSION

1. Explain in general the theory of good letterpress printing.

2. Name the four main factors which make makeready necessary.

3. Discuss the influence of paper surfaces on the necessity for makeready.

4. How does the nature of the job affect makeready?

5. Name the different materials from which a press form may be made.

6. What different conditions enter into the necessity to compensate for compression and stretch?

7. Why is it possible to eliminate practically all makeready in newspaper printing?

8. Discuss the work of multicolor presses.

9. What is meant by aniline printing? What printing surfaces are used in this method?

CHAPTER 23

Makeready Fundamentals

SUBJECT OUTLINE

A. Factors which influence the amount
   of makeready.
B. Preparing the form.
C. Making press adjustments.
D. Regulating the impression:
   1. Heavy.
   2. Light.

E. Marking out the sheet:
   1. Back.
   2. Front.
F. Patching the sheet.
G. Hanging the makeready or overlay
   sheet.

The topic for this chapter will comprise a general description of makeready methods rather than any specific makeready procedure. Makeready includes the various operations and adjustments necessary to prepare for the press run.

Several factors influence the amount of makeready required to prepare a job. Whether the makeready be simple or complicated depends entirely upon the job to be printed. Changing from one job to a similar one on the same press generally requires only simple preparation; but if the new job differs radically from the one previously run and requires many press adjustments, the makeready may be very complicated.

It has long been considered that if all equipment and conditions were perfect, no underlay or overlay would be required and the only makeready needed would be mechanical press adjustments to accommodate the various sizes of sheets being printed. If the form were in perfect condition, with all parts exactly type high, and the packing perfectly applied and free from wrinkles and lumps, the impression obtained should be perfect. However, such perfect conditions do not prevail. Certain printing surfaces may require more or less impression than others. In printing, these differences must be made up by underlay or overlay to regulate the pressure.

137

When a form is received by the pressman, he should inspect the plates and engravings to be sure they are all type high. If they are too low, the deficiency should not be adjusted by makeready on the cylinder, for if the circumference of the cylinder is increased by over-packing, the bed and the cylinder will not run in unison. Since the cylinder is designed to travel at the same speed as the bed, the form must be type high and the packing not much higher than the cylinder bearers.

If inspection of the plates discloses that they are too low, they should be underlaid; and if too high, they should be shaved down. The pressman should also make sure that the plates and engravings rest squarely on the bed, without rocking.

It is good practice, and one which will greatly simplify makeready, to keep all elements of the form as nearly type high as possible. This assures a minimum pressure of makeready on the cylinder, and minimum wear on the form. Packing should be kept free from lumps and wrinkles and just slightly above the height of the cylinder bearers. The printing press should be kept in the best possible condition. This is especially true of press parts which affect the register, such as bearers, grippers, register rack, air plungers, and guides. During the run, the impression should be just sufficient to transfer the ink evenly from the form to the paper.

A hard packing requires only a relatively light impression, which minimizes wear to both the form and the machine. Careful makeready prevents loss of time during the actual run, as no stops are required to make further press adjustments, to repair makeready, or to correct faulty inking conditions. Makeready should not be slighted except in extreme cases where rush work is being printed and proper makeready time is not allotted.

After the press is packed, the first step in makeready is to **prepare the form** properly. The bed, bearers, and back of the form should be cleaned carefully, and the form placed on the bed of the press, planed down, and carded. All parts of the form and chase must rest firmly on the bed of the press, so that all spring is eliminated. Then the form is locked on the bed of the press.

Next to be considered are the various **press adjustments**. In order to print properly, the cylinder and bed bearers must be in perfect contact at all times during the impression revolution of the cylinder. The press should be examined frequently by a machinist or a competent pressman to insure this. The sheet is positioned on the feedboard in such a way that the necessary mechanical adjustments will be kept at a minimum. The mechanical parts to be considered are those which are used for the actual printing and the delivery of the printed sheet.

Rollers should be in good condition and should be set properly. When the press is being inked for makeready, ink that does not dry quickly should be used and the quantity limited to that actually required for the makeready.

The next step in makeready is to pull a sheet and **regulate the amount of impression.** When a sheet is to be pulled for makeready, it should be placed to the guides just after the guides drop, the impression pulled, and the press stopped before the grippers release the sheet. The drop guides and feedboard are raised and the sheet stabbed while it is still held on the cylinder by the grippers, so that it may be replaced in the packing in register later. The sheet is removed and cut into as many sections as are required for convenience in handling, the size of the sections depending to a great extent on how closely the makeready must match the form.

An inspection of the back of the sheet will disclose any variations of the pressure of the form. As the sheet is marked out from the back, the impression should be sufficient to give a clear idea of the location of high and low areas. It is best to select an area with the correct amount of impression as a guide, and the low areas may then be built up accordingly. The first sheet checked usually shows excessive impression on small, isolated lines or pieces of type in some areas of the form. These may be disregarded, as they can be reduced during the makeready.

As a general rule, when but little time is allotted for makeready, a **heavier** impression than usual should be used. Another general rule is that, on long runs, it is best to use a hard packing and as light an impression as possible, to prevent wear on the form. It is generally conceded that book papers may be used in making ready jobs to be run on book stock. However, many pressmen prefer to use a lightweight sized and supercalendered stock for makeready purposes, as it gives a detailed impression, is less subject to shrinking or stretching, and is very good for areas which need to be lightened by scraping the surface of the paper.

The next step is to **mark out the sheet** from the back. In the pressroom, curtained markout booths are equipped with fluorescent lights mounted above an inclined board. Lights and boards for markout should be so arranged as to best show the impression. Sheets are marked either for tissue, which is about 0.001 inch in thickness, or for folio, which generally runs twice the thickness of tissue. (In the pressroom the term "folio" is generally applied to manifold stock 0.002 of an inch thick.)

Not more than three marks or spots for tissue or two for folio should be used, as anything beyond this range is sheer guesswork. The first and largest spot should include areas which need more impression to bring them to the required level. The second spot, which is marked inside the first, outlines areas that require still more impression. When marking out for tissue, the third spot should include areas which show no impression at all.

If sheets pulled for markout carried any pages or areas showing no impression at all, these areas should be underlaid or a printed sheet hung in the packing over them. Any area that requires two sheets of tissue can more easily be marked as a single sheet of folio, and the resulting makeready will probably be more effective. Areas that show excessive impression should be marked to be lightened, and the makeready sheet may be cut out at such points or scraped as needed.

After markout from the back has been completed, the sheet should be turned over and low areas or broken pieces of type marked out from the front. This may be accomplished by placing a piece of carbon paper, carbon side up, under the back of the sheet or by marking the space and putting the extra patches on the face.

The next step in makeready is to **patch the marked-out sheet.** This is an exacting job. Only the minimum of paste should be used and spread thinly and evenly. Marks in cutouts must be followed carefully.

The **made-ready or overlay sheet** is now hung carefully, with the stab marks in the packing and on the sheet in exact register. Paste should be applied near each stab mark and along the forward edge of the sheet, but not under printed areas. After the forward edge is pasted, the sheet is drawn taut and may be tipped to the packing along the back edge. In some cases, a second spot sheet may be required. Before it is marked out, however, a proof should be pulled and examined to see if the makeready is in correct position. Heavy impression in some areas may indicate a lump of paste or a folded-over piece of tissue or folio.

Sometimes, after the first makeready sheet has been hung in the packing, it becomes apparent that either slightly more or less impression is needed for proper printing. When a second spot sheet is required, it is marked out in the same manner as the first except that the face is very carefully examined to bring up every weak or broken letter. Two spot sheets will suffice for the general run of work handled in most pressrooms.

QUESTIONS FOR STUDY AND DISCUSSION

1. What are some factors which influence the amount of makeready needed for a job?

2. After the press has been packed, what is the next step in preparing for makeready?

3. What mechanical adjustments should be given consideration?

4. Describe the operation of pulling an impression sheet for makeready.

5. What will a study of the back of the impression sheet reveal?

6. When may a heavy impression be necessary?

7. When may a light impression be advisable? Why?

8. For what two grades of paper are impression sheets marked out?

9. In connection with makeready, what is meant by the term "folio"?

10. How many spots are marked for tissue? For folio?

11. What treatment is given an area which shows no impression? One which shows excessive impression?

12. What method may be used to mark out areas on the front of the sheets?

13. What precautions are necessary when the marked-out sheet is being patched?

14. Describe the process of hanging the makeready or overlay sheet.

CHAPTER 24

Makeready Underlay
and Interlay

SUBJECT OUTLINE

A. Definition of underlay and interlay.

B. Underlay:
1. Type forms.
2. Linotype slugs.
3. Plates on patent bases.
4. Block-mounted cuts and half-tones.

C. Interlay:
1. Block-mounted plates.
2. Plates on patent bases.

D. Plugging quoins.

E. Advantages of underlay and interlay:
1. Bring form to type height.
2. Save time.
3. Avoid overpacking of cylinder.
4. Decrease plate wear.

In most commercial shops, plates are made from 0.005 to 0.006 of an inch below type height to allow for underlay and interlay. In the Government Printing Office, however, plates are made 0.159 of an inch thick; and when this measurement is added to the height of a patent base, 0.759 of an inch, it gives 0.918 of an inch, which is standard type height. Because of this, the use of underlay or interlay in this class of work is not practiced in some sections of the Office.

Exact measurements to bring all parts of a form to exactly type height are the goal, but this goal is not always achieved, and it is then that underlay or interlay provides speedy and satisfactory makeready. Underlay and interlay may be defined as follows: Underlay is the means used to bring the form, whether it be patent-base-mounted plates, block-mounted plates, or type, to type height or 0.918 of an inch, and to equalize the impression; while interlay is the means used to level the surface of individual cuts or plates. The amount of underlay needed is determined by measuring the plate or type with a micrometer or type-high gage, while the interlay is marked out from the impression seen on the back of a printed sheet.

143

Let us first consider the underlay. On type forms underlay is seldom used, as most types are within a few thousandths of an inch of type height. On small forms, however, large letters may be worn so much that they are not properly inked, and these must be underlaid. Sometimes sections of type forms such as large letters or solids require more impression. Such forms are underlaid to prevent the packing from becoming lumpy or overpacked.

When **linotype slugs** are low on one end they may be underlaid on short runs, but for long runs the slug should be replaced. If all the units were exactly type high in a form composed of solid and light sections, the extra pressure needed to print the solid areas would have to be applied under the packing, which would cause overpacking the cylinder and result in poor printing.

When **plates to be used on patent bases** are to be gaged, a small section of the patent base should be at hand and the plates measured individually on this section by use of the type-high gage. This is done in the same manner as that described for block-mounted plates, the exception being that any sheets to be added as underlay are placed loosely between the base and the plate.

Let us consider that a form composed of many **block-mounted cuts or halftones** has been delivered to the pressroom from the Composing Division locked within a chase. The form is placed either on a stone or on the bed of the press, the quoins unlocked, and the height of the cuts measured with the type-high gage. When a cut is removed from the form, the gripper edge should be marked with chalk to insure proper repositioning, and care must be exercised in the use of the gage to avoid damaging it. If the cuts are below type height, various thicknesses of paper are added. To gage their height, a sheet of paper is first placed between the gage and the printing surface of the cuts to protect them from possible damage from the micrometer or type-high gage. If a cut is 0.003 of an inch low, a piece of stock similar to sized and supercalendered paper, which is about 0.003 of an inch thick, would be sufficient to bring it to type height.

After the correct measurement is ascertained, the paper is trimmed to the size of the cut and pasted to the bottom of the wood block, and the block replaced in its proper position in the form. Each cut within the form is gaged similarly. Very heavy cuts or solids may be underlaid so as to be slightly more than type high, perhaps 0.003 of an inch higher. Those with delicate highlights or with edges that fade away when printed, commonly known as vignettes, should be slightly less than type high. If a cut is found to be more than type high, the block should be shaved or sandpapered down to the proper height.

Large block-mounted cuts are seldom used in our Office, but when one is used, a check should be made to determine whether or not it is warped. This may be done by the use of a straightedge on the surface of the plates, care being exercised to avoid scratching the plate surface. Warped cuts should be replaned or sandpapered to make them level; or, if they are too badly warped, they should be remounted.

After the preliminary underlay has been completed, the form is locked up, correctly placed on the bed, and the first impression pulled. The printing is positioned properly on the sheet, and this OK or positioning sheet is submitted to the reviser. While the pressman waits for the return of this sheet, he may proceed with the final underlay. When the impression is checked, it may be found that several of the block-mounted plates are slightly low and one or two slightly high. If this condition exists, the form is unlocked and the necessary changes made. The high plates are sandpapered down, and additional paper is added under the blocks of the low ones to give the even impression needed for good printing.

The next step is to prepare for the interlay whenever it is needed. Block-mounted plates are not usually interlaid, but sometimes it may be necessary. The back of the sheet is first marked out and all dark or solid areas in the plate given additional printing pressure. When plates are correctly interlaid, the rollers will ink the form properly and very little makeready will be required under the packing. Much care is needed to remove the plate from the woodblock. The tacks which hold the plate to the base or block are carefully pried from the edge of the plate with a screwdriver or other tool, or the bottom of the block is hit on a level surface to loosen the brads. Care must be used to avoid bending the plate. The plate is removed from the block and the tack holes carefully filed level.

When the plate is to be remounted, new holes must be made in both the plate and the block. The interlay which has been prepared and spotted is then mounted or pasted to the back of the plate, printed side out. Care must be used to ensure proper positioning of the interlay, which may be done best by the use of calipers. When it is properly positioned, the sheet is matched up with the plate by alining a predetermined section of both the plate and the interlay sheet. A light film of paste should be used to fasten the sheet to the back of the plate. The plate is then remounted on the base or block. To do this, two of the tacks that had been removed are driven lightly part way into the old holes to assure proper positioning of the plate. New holes for the remaining tacks are then started by the use of the pointed center punch. The tacks are driven in as far as possible with a hammer and then a nail set is used. The cut should then be checked to make sure it is type high and correctly positioned in the form.

It is a common practice to interlay **plates** when they are used **on patent bases**. This is not difficult and is very effective in successful makeready. Only the general areas should be marked out for interlays. Small patches are not effective or necessary, since in many cases they would probably come right in the groove of the base and would have no effect on the printing impression. By this time, the OK or positioning sheet should have been returned, so the plates may be interlaid and all the moves necessary to obtain accurate register made at the same time.

Plates on patented bases are interlaid in the same manner as those mounted on wooden blocks. The interlay is much simpler, because in order to remove the plates from the base it is necessary only to loosen the blocks or catches on two sides, instead of removing the plates from the blocks. The interlay is then positioned in the same manner by the use of calipers or by alining the surface with the printed part on the interlay. Paste should not be used exclusively.

For example, a book form may contain 16 pages on the bed, the plates imposed and underlaid, a sheet positioned and sent for OK, and another sheet pulled for interlay. The gripper edge of the sheet should be marked with an X at each bottom guide; then, starting with the plate on the printed sheet nearest the bottom guides and the control or near side of the press, the pages should be numbered 1, 2, 3, 4, across the sheet. The second line from the gripper edge, also starting from the near side of the press, will be numbered 5, 6, 7, 8, the third line 9, 10, 11, 12, and the back row of plates 13, 14, 15, 16. This may be done either on the cylinder press feedboard or on a table. The plates on the base must correspond with these numbers and may be more easily worked by folding the marked sheet in the middle so that two plate rows may be interlaid at the same time.

A definite and habit-forming procedure should be developed in the removal of plates from the base. In one procedure practiced widely, the catches in the center or folding margins are left in place, as are those at the heads of the plates. The remaining plate catches at the trim edge of the plates and at the foot are loosened enough to permit plate removal. In a form similar to that used as an example, this would mean that all the outside catches of the form and both centerlines of catches between each two rows of plates should be loosened.

Many pressmen form the good habit of marking the base with chalklines to indicate which catches were loosened or are to be loosened. This is a great help, and it is recommended that apprentices form this habit during the training period. When the plates have been removed and interlaid, and all plate moves made that are necessary to obtain accurate register, they may be relocked to the base. This completes the primary makeready operations.

Before the press run is started on forms locked within a chase or a patented base mounted on the bed of the press, the quoins should be plugged with wet paper. Small plugs of paper are placed in the exposed edges of the quoins; that is, between two quoins in their locked position, and driven in firmly by the use of the edge of a quoin key or a small hammer. After the quoins have been plugged in this manner, their position is marked by a chalkline drawn across the quoins and each adjacent piece of furniture. This insures correct positioning of the quoins again, if it should become necessary to unlock them for any further work on the form.

Finally the **advantages of underlay and interlay** should be considered. They **bring the entire form to type height,** which is the proper height for good printing, since the rollers must touch and ink the entire form evenly. Much **time is saved,** as partial makeready may be made before the positioning OK sheet is returned. **Overpacking of the cylinder is avoided,** and this eliminates many packing troubles which generally occur during the run, among them being the tendency of the packing to creep or to pull away from the packing clamps. **Less plate wear** is experienced if the plates are properly underlaid. This is noticeable on long runs and when the plates are used many times. The importance of underlay and interlay cannot be overlooked, and some of the most successful pressmen use this method of makeready to good advantage.

QUESTIONS FOR STUDY AND DISCUSSION

1. Define the terms "underlay" and "interlay."
2. On type forms, what conditions sometimes require the application of underlay?
3. When should linotype slugs be underlaid and when replaced?
4. How may the height of block-mounted cuts or halftones be gaged?
5. Describe the process of underlaying block-mounted cuts and halftones.
6. What method is used to gage the height of plates to be printed on patent bases?
7. What special check should be given large block-mounted cuts?
8. When is the first OK or positioning sheet pulled and submitted to the reviser?

9. What work may be done by the pressman while waiting for the return of the OK proof?

10. Discuss the process of applying interlay to block-mounted plates.

11. How are plates which are to be run on patent bases interlaid?

12. What widely practiced procedure is followed when removing plates from patent bases?

13. What good method is often used to mark patent bases where catches have been loosened to remove plates?

14. What is meant by "plugging quoins"?

15. Discuss some of the advantages of the use of underlay and interlay.

CHAPTER 25

Makeready Overlay

SUBJECT OUTLINE

A. Definition of overlay:
B. The pitch line.
C. The sheet to be used for overlay.
    1. Pulling the sheet.
    2. Numbering the sections.

3. Separating the sections.
4. Marking out areas.
5. Spotting up areas.
6. Hanging the sections.
D. Important things to remember.

The previous chapter dealt with underlay and interlay and, if these have been properly done, the form should be level. After the sheet has been correctly positioned, the lineup returned OK, and all moves necessary to obtain correct register made, the form is ready for the overlay.

The term "overlay" may be defined as that part of the makeready which is carried within the packing to give the various parts of the form the even impression required for proper printing. The overlay consists of a makeready sheet which has been spotted with tissue, folio, or the same kind of paper as that used for the overlay itself.

Let us first consider the pitch line which indicates the travel between the sheet to be printed and the printing surface of the form and refers to an imaginary line on which two contacting gears travel together at the same speed. If the cylinder is properly packed and the form is exactly type high, the printing surface and the paper being printed should run together evenly. If too many sheets are carried on the packing, resulting in overpacking, the circumference of the cylinder will be greater than it should be. Therefore, the packing will have a tendency to move faster than the form during printing and will pull away from the packing clamps. The opposite condition will exist if the cylinder is underpacked, as the form will then move faster than the packing which will creep or pull away from the reel or tail end. It is essential to good presswork that the correct pitch line should be maintained.

149

Usually less ink is needed to print a sheet for overlay than when the job itself is being printed. As the press will be standing for short periods of time while the sheet is marked out and patched up, ink that will not dry on the press should be used. Since at this stage the work of underlay and interlay has been completed, the impression to be seen from the back of the sheet should now be satisfactory, and a sheet for overlay may be pulled. The speed of the press should not be too high when this sheet is being pulled, and the press should be run until the bottom or drop guides are just positioned on the guide tongues. Then the sheet is placed to both the bottom and the side guides, the trip released, and the machine started with the left hand on the control and the right foot on the press brake. Just as the impression is completed but before the grippers release the sheet, the brake is applied. At this stage, the sheet is fully printed but still retained by the grippers, and may be stabbed on the cylinder.

Let us assume a sheet size 24 by 38 inches is to be used. The best way to work this size is to mark it into sections and number the sections, No. 1 for the part nearest the control side and No. 2 for the far side of the sheet. Larger sheets, or those with many half-tones, must be marked into four or more sections. Both ends of each section should be stabbed by a makeready knife, an awl, or similar instrument. The makeready knife should be held at right angles to the surface of the cylinder and should not be thrust into the packing deep enough to reach and damage the metal surface of the cylinder. When the makeready knife is used, two slits must be made at an angle to form an open V, such as \/. When an awl is used, a single stab will suffice. The press is then run forward, and the sheet removed from the cylinder.

The sheet is laid on a table or other suitable surface and folded with the printed side out to form the sections already marked. Three-eighths of an inch of paper is cut from the gripper margin, and the marked sections separated by cutting through the folded sheet ⅛ of an inch from the folded edge. The strip of paper thus removed from the folded edge is ¼ of an inch wide in all. The sections are then taken to the markout board and the angle of the board adjusted so the impression on the back or unprinted side may be seen.

The first glance at the impression shows that on some areas the impression is too heavy while on others it is too light. The part of the impression which appears to be about right is selected, and the purpose of marking out is to make all the impression correspond to that part. When a low area is to be marked out, its outline should be considered. If the center of a page is low and the outside edges are just right, the low places are marked out, the first spot being marked up to the edge where the impression is as desired. All areas that are just a little low should be included in this mark or outline. Inside this outline, some of the printed matter will have sufficient impression to be heavy enough with just this one sheet.

The next spot is marked inside the first to include all the type that is just a little lower than that on the inside edge of the first mark. In some cases it may be necessary to put three spots on certain sections to bring them to proper height. At no time, however, should more than three spots be used.

Actual experience is necessary to mark out an overlay successfully. Any high spots which appear on the impression may be cut out completely or relieved by scraping the surface of the sheet at this high spot. There are several methods of doing this, one of which is to scrape the surface of the paper with the edge of the makeready knife. Care must be used while scraping the surface of the sheet to avoid tearing it.

Now that the overlay is marked out, it is ready to be spotted up. The material used for spotting up may be tissue, which is about 0.001 of an inch thick; folio, which is about 0.002 of an inch thick; or book paper, which is 0.003 of an inch thick. If tissue is to be used as the spotting-up medium, it is not necessary to indicate its use by a specific mark; if folio is wanted, the letter "F" is used within the outline for all spots requiring folio; and book paper is indicated by the letter "B." If some sheets are to be spotted up by using all folio, "all F" is written either within the spot or at some convenient point on the sheet; and any area that is to be cut out is marked by the letter "X." When the sheet is spotted up, these symbols must be followed.

Spotting is usually done on a flat-top zinc-covered table. A carefully sharpened makeready knife is needed and a can of paste set on a piece of cardboard, or a dab of paste may be carried on the back of the left hand as is generally done by most pressmen. The paste is applied to the spots in a thin even film by the second finger of the right hand, the makeready knife being held between the thumb and first finger. The smallest or inner area is spotted up first. The paste is spread thin, without lumps, and the paper to be used is positioned over the spot.

If a soft black pencil has been used to mark out the sheet for overlay, the outline of the spot will appear clearly through the paper. The paper is cut around this outline to the edge of the mark, care being taken to avoid cutting through the overlay sheet. Then the next largest area is spotted and, finally, the outside or largest marks. All necessary cutouts are also made at this time. Attention is then given to the stab marks already made on the overlay. If slits have been cut to form the two sides of an open V, this small triangle of paper may be cut out completely, or a dog ear may be made by which the overlay is matched to the slits in the packing.

The press is run and the reel which holds the tail end of the temporary packing top sheet brought into place. This reel is loosened by using the pin wrench, the press is run to a position which brings the front or clamped edge of the packing into view while the grippers are open, and the shooflies are raised by the use of a pin wrench. The top sheet and four or five white hangers are lifted and, after a sheet of the same weight as that being added is dropped from the packing, the overlay sheet may be positioned.

The two sections of the overlay sheet are now ready to be hung within the packing, with section 1 on the control side of the press and section 2 on the far or gear side of the packing. A light film of paste is applied along the top or gripper edge of section 2, the stab marks matched with those on the packing, and this section hung firmly in place. The same method is used to hang section 1, the packing is closed, and the tail end reeled in.

The feedboard is lowered and another sheet pulled to see what results have been achieved. The impression should be fairly even by this time, although some forms will require a second spot sheet. If a second spot sheet is necessary, it need not be stabbed. The sections are marked out from the back, particular attention being paid to the printed side or face, which is carefully examined and any weak letters or printing marked and spotted up. The sections are spotted up as before, trimmed in the same manner, and hung in the packing directly over the first overlay by cutting dog ears at the edge of the print and matching the second overlay to the first. When a second spot sheet is necessary, another sheet must be dropped from the packing to make allowance for it.

The makeready overlay has now been completed. Any other spots that are required for the impression may be applied directly to the face of the overlay sheet. The experience necessary to successfully mark out an overlay comes only through practice and the apprentice should profit by his mistakes as he goes along. The **important things to remember are:** Use a soft black pencil for marking out, have the makeready knife sharp while patching up, use care in following the outline with the knife, spread the paste thinly and evenly to avoid lumps which cause uneven impressions, do not apply more than three spots to any single overlay, and hang the makeready sheet so that the stab marks aline.

QUESTIONS FOR STUDY AND DISCUSSION

1. Define the term "overlay."

2. What is the pitch line? Why is it important to good presswork?

3. What kind of ink should be used to print the sheet for overlay? Why?

4. Describe the process of pulling the sheet to be used for overlay.

5. Why is the sheet for overlay marked into sections? How are the stab marks made?

6. After the sheet has been removed from the cylinder, what procedure is followed to separate the sections?

7. What is the purpose of marking out low areas on the overlay sheet?

8. How many spots may be marked for low areas?

9. What kinds of paper are used to spot up the overlay sheet?

10. How is the kind of paper to be used indicated on the overlay sheet?

11. What other materials besides paper are needed in spotting up?

12. Describe the work of hanging the overlay sheet within the packing.

13. If a second spot sheet is necessary, what precaution should be taken to make allowance for it in the packing?

14. Discuss some important things to remember when an overlay sheet is being prepared and hung in the packing.

CHAPTER 26

Mechanism of Cylinder Presses—Feeding Unit

SUBJECT OUTLINE

A. The feedboard:
1. Regulating height.
2. Adjusting to counteract warping.
3. Placing guide tongues.
4. Positioning the side guide.

B. Front guides:
1. Setting to tongues.
2. Adjusting sheet guards.
3. Timing.
C. Grippers.
D. Bands.
E. Brush.
F. Manila apron.

This is the first of a group of three chapters in which the feeding, printing, and delivery units of cylinder presses will be considered. In the discussion of the feeding unit, attention is directed first to the **feedboard.** The feedboard is made of wood and is inclined at a slight angle toward the guides and hinged in the center. The forward end may be raised to facilitate the process of packing the cylinder, and on hand-fed presses the back end may be raised while the operator is working on the form on the bed of the press. A metal strip about 6 inches wide extends across the front or guide edge of the feedboard. The guide tongues are attached under this strip, and the side guide is usually positioned to holes in this strip to facilitate hand feeding.

Two adjustments may be made to the feedboard. The first adjustment **regulates the height** of the feedboard above the packing. This is done by placing a straightedge on the feedboard with the end of the straightedge extending over the cylinder bearer. The height of the feedboard is adjusted by turning the thumbscrews under each corner of the board until the front edge of the board is about ¼₆ of an inch below the top of the cylinder bearers. After the height has been set, the locknuts on the thumbscrews are tightened.

If the feedboard has become **warped, a second adjustment may be made** to raise or lower the center of the board by changing the length of the bridged iron rod which extends to both sides near the front of the board. It is easy to decide whether or not the feedboard has become warped by placing a straightedge on top of the board.

The **guide tongues** extend over the cylinder beyond the edge of the feedboard and are about 3 inches long and ¾ of an inch wide. These guide tongues should be about $\frac{1}{32}$ of an inch above the top sheet of the packing and curved to fit the cylinder. They are fitted to a slide on the underside of the feedboard. They should slide freely, but not loosely, and when positioned, they should clear the grippers and shooflies on the cylinder. Guide tongues which are set too high will cause wrinkles, slurs, and inaccurate register.

The **positioning of the side guide** needs no explanation at this time, but its face should be square with the edge of the sheet.

When the **front guides** are correctly positioned to a small sheet, it should be balanced and supported by the guides. The accepted method of setting the front guides on large sheets is to fold the sheet in the center, end to end, and then make another parallel fold, thus making three crosswise creases. The sheet is then unfolded, placed to the guides, and the tongues positioned to the two outside folds.

When the front guides are to be **set to the tongues,** the press is run until the guides just drop. The guide thumbscrews are loosened, the guide rod lowered to its lowest position, one front guide tightened in an upward position on the rod, and the other set to the guide tongue.

The raised guide is then loosened and also set to the tongue. The bottom of the guides should be square with the guide tongues and centered on them. The faces of the guides must be square with the positioned sheet, and the guides must not depress the tongues. The operator should not lean on the feedboard while he is setting the guides.

The next step is to **adjust the sheet guards.** These are two small metal pieces on the face of each guide which hold the sheet close to the tongues and prevent the forward edge of the sheet from curling up or down. The sheet guards may be bent to make this adjustment.

Correct timing of the guides is necessary. If they are timed to rise too late, the grippers will grasp the sheet and tear the front edge before the guides fully release it. If the guides are timed to rise too soon, there is too long a period of time when neither the grippers nor the guides control the position of the sheet, which causes poor register. The press is run until the grippers close to within ¼ to ⅜ of an inch of the packing. The lifting finger is loosened on the far end of the guide rod and pressed down against the lifting pin. The setscrew is tightened and the setting of the front guides completed.

The grippers carry the sheet from the feedboard around the cylinder on impression and deliver it from the cylinder. The gripper setting should be checked regularly, especially before a long run or one which requires close register. The setting of the grippers should not be attempted until the makeready has been completed and all spot sheets hung in the packing. The gripper squeeze or pressure on the top sheet is regulated by tension springs in the gripper mechanism. The grippers should all have the same relative curve, and the ends or edges which bite the sheet should form a straight line. They should be free on the shaft so that they may be moved readily. The application of cup grease or the use of emery paper will free the grippers on the shaft.

The press is run until the grippers close fully, and their position is marked on the packing. A piece of paper 0.010 of an inch thick is placed between the gripper tumbler and the tumbler stop, which is on the gear side of the cylinder. All the grippers on the shaft are loosened and set one at a time while a piece of the stock to be run is placed between the gripper and the packing. The extreme end of the gripper should be pressed firmly where it extends over the packing and the setscrew tightened lightly and carefully.

After all grippers have been set, the setscrews on each one are tightened firmly, and the paper removed from between the tumbler and the stop. An even holding tension may be applied to each gripper by this method. Better register will be obtained and less trouble encountered if the sheets slip slightly from the grippers instead of being held too tightly on impression.

Across the press, in front of the cylinder, are a series of bands which hold the sheet to the cylinder before it is printed. These bands should be spaced so that one comes between each two grippers. They are curved to conform to the curve of the cylinder, and their purpose is to smooth the air from under the sheet before it is printed. Tight bands on the ends of the cylinder will cause the stock to wrinkle, and a tight band anywhere on the cylinder will mark the sheet. With the cylinder down on impression, the center bands are set so that they clear the packing by the thickness of two or three sheets of manila paper. The outer bands should be set slightly farther away from the cylinder than the center bands. A band should never be set over a gripper or sheet lifter. The sheet lifter will be discussed in the next chapter.

Most cylinder presses are equipped with a brush which helps to hold the sheet against the cylinder before impression, to press out the air, and to smooth the wrinkles in the paper. The setting of the brush may be checked by placing the ends of three long narrow strips of paper into the grippers. One of the strips is placed on the center of the cylinder and the others on each end. The cylinder is turned on impression and stopped when the grippers are seen from the back of the press. If a form is on the press, the impression line should be on a margin. The ends of the strips should then be released by tumbling the grippers with a pin wrench. Now the tension of the brush may be tested by pulling on the strips of paper. The brush should be adjusted from both sides of the press and set slightly tighter in the center than on the ends, as this will smooth the sheet and prevent wrinkles. If the brush is slightly low in the center, it should be underlaid.

A manila apron is sometimes used to obtain register on certain jobs. This apron is placed in the press so as to come between the bands and brush and the cylinder. Besides allowing the bands and brush to be set tighter without marking the sheet, the apron also prevents the corners of the gripper edge of the sheet from being turned over by the brush. Even when such an apron is used, the bands should not be set tight enough to pull the sheet from the grippers while it is being printed. The apron must be anchored firmly to the press. If it should break loose while the press is running, the type or plates of the form may be battered.

The manila sheet should be measured from the rod which holds the bands to a point beyond the brush but not far enough to touch the form and allowing 4 inches extra for the overlap. If the apron touches the form, it will be pulled off with the first impression. A fold is made in the apron at the point where it will be attached to the band rod. The feedboard of the press is raised, and, with the lip or 4-inch overlap turned upward toward the front of the press, the manila sheet is passed between the bands and the cylinder. The fold of the sheet is pressed down on the band setscrews until they break through. After all setscrews across the press are pushed through the fold, the sheet is more firmly secured in place by tightening a noose in the end of a string over one end setscrew and passing a loop around each screw across the press. The string is then tied to the setscrew at the other side of the band rod, and the apron is in place. This apron is not to be confused with the apron stretched below the tapes to protect the form, rollers, and inking table from dust, torn sheets, and broken tapes.

Let us now summarize the adjustment of these mechanisms needed to produce good printing. The feedboard must be set to the correct height, the guides must be square and must rise at the correct time, all grippers must be set accurately and have equal tension, and the bands and brush must be set so as to remove the air and wrinkles from the sheet. All these adjustments are essential to the proper handling of the sheet on impression.

QUESTIONS FOR STUDY AND DISCUSSION

1. Describe the feedboard on cylinder presses.
2. How may the height of the feedboard be adjusted?
3. If the feedboard becomes warped, how may the condition be remedied?
4. Discuss the correct position for the guide tongues.
5. Describe the process of setting the front guides to the tongues.
6. How are the sheet guards adjusted?
7. Why is accurate timing of the guides essential?
8. What is the function of the grippers?
9. Discuss the process of setting the grippers.
10. What is the purpose of the bands?
11. How may the setting of the brush be tested? How may the tension be adjusted?
12. What is the function of the manila apron used for some jobs? How is it placed in correct position?

CHAPTER 27

Mechanism of Cylinder Presses—Printing Unit

SUBJECT OUTLINE

A. Power control:
    1. Older style electric control.
    2. Later control methods.
B. Foot pedals:
    1. Brake.
    2. Trip.
C. Printing unit:
    1. Bed:
        a. Gibs.

        b. Bearers.
        c. Register rack.
        d. Airheads.
    2. Cylinder:
        a. Lift springs.
        b. Packing clamp.
        c. Reels.

First, let us thoroughly understand the **power control** of the cylinder press. The control device, the press brake, and the trip pedal are on the feeder or control side of the press. The older style electric control device has a handle which extends about 4 inches from a curved metal control box. It is equipped with hinged latches which hold the handle in any one of three positions. When the handle is in the central or neutral position, the press will not run and is on the safe position. When the handle is in the uppermost position, the press will run forward, and the speed must be regulated directly from the control box. When the handle is in the lowermost position, the press will reverse. The press should be backed only when absolutely necessary, as much damage may be caused by improper backing.

In later **control methods** the panel is on the side of the press with separate buttons for each operation. There is a button for each of the following movements: to run the press continuously forward; to inch or jog the press forward, that is, to move it only a small distance forward; to reverse the press by inching; and to stop it. In many cases the speed control is mounted on the same panel.

The platform on which the pressman stands to run or feed the press has two foot pedals. The foot pedal toward the front of the press is the brake. The press is brought to a stop by shutting off the power and applying pressure to the brake, which may be locked in its downward position by depressing it and pushing it toward the front of the press. The trip pedal is toward the rear of the press. This pedal also may be locked down and, when it is in that position, the cylinder stays in a raised or off-impression position. The press should never be started without first looking over the bed, the feedboard, and the joggerboard to make sure that there is nothing loose which may fall into the press while it is running. The pressman should also make sure that no other person is working around the press before he pushes the run button.

The printing unit includes the cylinder, the bed, and the machinery necessary to drive, control, and support these parts. The cylinder and bed must travel together to insure proper printing.

Let us first consider the bed of the press. This is a flat, even surface on which the form is placed for printing. It is supported by four roller tracks spaced evenly across the press. Four bed gibs are attached by lock screws near each of the four corners of the bed to prevent sidewise movement of the bed itself. While the bed is in motion, these gibs ride on the edge of the bed roller tracks. If the gibs become worn or loosened, adjustment is very simple. After the screw has been loosened, the gib is held alongside the roller track and then tightened against it with 0.002 of an inch clearance. After the gibs have been adjusted, they should be watched. If they show a tendency to overheat, they have been set too tight. They should be oiled daily and have a small oil recess or well on their upper side for that purpose.

On each side of the bed are the bed bearers which run the entire length of the bed and are about 2 inches wide. A chart was included in one of the earlier chapters and from it we find that the bed bearers on most Miehle presses are generally 0.9167 of an inch high, but on some presses they are 0.914 of an inch high. At no time should they be above standard type height. Bed bearers that have become worn may be underlaid by the machinists until they are the proper height but should be replaced as soon as possible. They should always be kept clean and wiped twice a day during press runs, and the screws holding them to the bed should be inspected regularly and kept tight.

The register rack is bolted to the side of the bed on the control side of the press. Its purpose is to insure perfect register between the cylinder and the bed while the press is on impression. Usually this rack is adjusted by the pressman. The proper method is to mark the position of the rack, loosen the bolts just enough to permit moving the rack, and turn the press over on impression until the center teeth of the rack come into contact or mesh with the center teeth of the segment on the cylinder. Then the pressman tries to move the rack and, if there is any play between the teeth of the rack and segment, shims are inserted under the rack. Shims of greater thickness than 0.002 of an inch should not be placed under the rack at any one time. As each shim is added, the rack is positioned again to see if any play still exists. After all play has been eliminated, the screws are tightened slightly and the press is run on impression 8 or 10 times. By this means the rack is moved by the segment on the cylinder to its proper position. Then the rack screws are tightened and the adjustment is complete.

On each end of the bed are one or two airheads. On the newer Miehle presses these are of the metal piston-ring type and need no adjustment. On the older presses, however, the airheads are equipped with leather cups which create sufficient pressure when entering the cylinder chamber to slow up the motion of the bed. The adjustment of these airheads is complicated and will not be discussed at this time. However, the leather on the airheads should be treated at least once a month with neat's-foot oil. The leather should be kept free from any other kind of oil, as other kinds are injurious to the leather. The airheads slow up the motion of the bed as it comes to the end of its forward or backward motion and also helps to start the bed traveling in the opposite direction. Miehle presses have the direct-drive bed motion. Besides regular oiling, this mechanism requires little attention.

The cylinder which carries the packing and the sheet to be printed has two adjustments, one of which should be checked frequently, while the other seldom, if ever, needs attention. The setting of the cylinder to the bed is really a machinist's job, but all pressmen should know how to make this adjustment. It is always necessary that the cylinder and the bed bearers run together. Proper adjustment of the cylinder to the bed will insure this. If the bed or cylinder bearers or bearings become worn, or if heavy forms are run continuously, the cylinder and bed bearers may lose contact with each other.

When the cylinder is pulled down to the bed by the machinist, the form and bed bearers must be removed first. However, it is sometimes necessary, while the press is running, to pull the cylinder down while the form is still on the press. This is accomplished in the following manner: With the cylinder off impression, the impression nuts, located just above the floor directly below the cylinder on each side, are turned about the width of one hole which is about a quarter of an inch. This will move the cylinder down from 0.002 to 0.003 of an inch. The locknuts are then tightened, and the form is printed on impression. After any cylinder adjustments have been made, the press should be turned over on impression by turning the flywheel by hand. On very heavy forms, however, this cannot be done.

The cylinder **lift springs** lift the cylinder from the bed after impression. If the cylinder does not lift properly after impression, these springs need to be adjusted. Two setscrews adjust the tension of the springs. These are loosened, the block supporting the tension springs is raised on the level, and the setscrews locked again. There should be just enough tension on these springs to lift the cylinder, as too much tension will cause excessive wear. This adjustment is made on each side of the machine.

The cylinder **packing clamps** hold the packing in place on the packing pins. The number varies, depending on the width of the cylinder. Their proper setting can be learned best by demonstration and experience. As all the clamps are mounted on the same rod running crosswise of the cylinder, allowance must be made for the twist of this rod. First, all the clamps are loosened and the packing clamp lever on the control side of the press is opened about 1 inch. This opening must be maintained while the clamps are being set. Then the two on the extreme end or gear side of the press are set up against the packing and their setscrews tightened. The third clamp from the gear side of the press is then set with 0.005 of an inch clearance between the clamp and the packing. As we move toward the control side of the press, setting the remaining clamps, 0.005 of an inch is added for each succeeding clamp set. That is, the fourth would have 0.01 of an inch clearance; the fifth, 0.015; the sixth, 0.020; and so on until all have been set. The packing lever should now be placed in the locked position, and the adjustment of the packing clamps is completed.

The cylinder also contains two **reels** which are used to reel in the tail end of the packing top sheets. These reels need no adjustment. The cylinder itself may also be moved ahead, so that oversized forms may be accommodated on the bed of the press. This allows the forms to be positioned on the bed so that the type surface extends beyond the deadline. In the cylinder gear on the far side of the press are three series of holes, with a screw in the first hole of each of the three series. In order to advance the cylinder, these screws must be removed and the ring gear shifted to the next hole or farther, as desired. The cylinder is advanced approximately ¾ of an inch for each hole.

QUESTIONS FOR STUDY AND DISCUSSION

1. Describe the power control of cylinder presses.
2. Where is the brake located? The trip pedal?
3. What are the two principal parts of the printing unit?
4. Describe the bed of the press.
5. Where are the bed gibs located? What is their function?
6. What care should be given the bed bearers?
7. What is the purpose of the register rack? How is it adjusted?
8. Where are the airheads located? What is their purpose? What care should be given them?
9. By what means is the cylinder lifted from the bed after impression?
10. How is the packing held in place?
11. How is the tail of the packing reeled in?
12. By what means is the cylinder advanced?

CHAPTER 28

Mechanism of Cylinder Presses—Feeder and Delivery Units

SUBJECT OUTLINE

A. The feeder unit:
    1. History.
    2. Loading board or elevator.
    3. Combing wheels.
    4. Suction lifter.
B. Stream feeder.
C. The continuous feeder:
    1. Wooden cylinder.
    2. Heavy canvas tapes.
    3. Combing wheels.
    4. Forwarding wheels.
    5. Slowdown devices.
D. Grippers.

E. Sheet lifters or shooflies.
F. Stripper fingers.
G. Tape pulleys.
H. Two delivery methods:
    1. Face-up slide delivery.
    2. Face-down delivery.
I. The chain delivery conveyor.
J. Automatic delivery.
K. Joggers.
L. Miscellaneous delivery parts:
    1. Star wheels.
    2. Driving wheels.
    3. Slitting attachment.

With the improvements made in printing presses, the speed became too great for them to be fed by hand. Feeding was no problem on web presses which are fed from a roll, but on those presses delivery was a problem. Anyone who has fed presses by hand knows that it is physically tiresome, monotonous, and a nervous strain to stand in the same place, for the same work, hour after hour.

In an 8-hour day of feeding a cylinder press by hand, at least $1\frac{1}{2}$ hours are spent in placing lifts of paper on the feedboard and in combing and rolling out the stock preliminary to feeding the press. This amounts to a loss of production of about 2,000 sheets during an 8-hour day.

167

Numerous experiments in the development of automatic feeders were tried in the latter part of the 19th century but most of them were not successful. It is believed that the first successful pile feeder came into use in the very last part of that century. Pile feeders consist of a loading board or elevator on the feedboard end of the press on which thousands of sheets are stocked at once. They may be loaded by hand or as the paper is delivered in an even pile from the factory. The top of the pile is kept at constant height by mechanical means.

The sheets are separated and aired in much the same manner as that employed by the hand feeders. Some feeders incorporate small combing wheels which separate the sheets at the corners. They are located on the back edge of the sheet at each corner. The more modern feeders have a suction lifter in place of the combers to separate the sheets. The corners of the top sheet on the pile are lifted by a suction device and air is blown under the whole sheet by small air nozzles located near the suction lifters. The sheet is then sent forward by suction devices located either forward on the sheet or along the back edge of the sheet and the sheet is carried forward to the forwarding rollers.

Most modern presses incorporate the stream feeder principle, which greatly simplifies the problems of feeding high-speed presses. Each sheet fed to the forwarding rollers is partially overlapped by the one which was above it in the pile and which now precedes it down the tapes to the guides. Instead of a single sheet moving swiftly and alone to the guides there is now a stream of sheets, each one overlapped on its front edge by the one preceding it. This is a great improvement in that curled stock can be more easily run because the front edge of the sheet is kept from curling up on its speedy trip down the tapes. In this method of feeding, about seven sheets are in motion down the tapes continually, therefore, tape speeds have been considerably slowed.

Control of the sheet is taken over by the forwarding wheels after leaving the pile and release by the suction devices. It is then eased to the guides by a series of tapes and slowdown devices on some presses, pulled mechanically to the side guide, and perfect register is assured.

The pile is raised automatically as sheets are fed from it and several safety devices prevent damage to the form or press when improper feeding occurs. These safety devices mechanically trip or throw off the press when more than one sheet is delivered from the pile at once, when the sheet is not properly positioned to the front guides, or when it jams on delivery from the cylinder. There are many different kinds of pile feeders which handle any paper printable by the various cylinder presses. Their only fault is the time lost in reloading the pile.

In the continuous-feed machine the press need not be stopped to reload as the paper supply can be replenished while the press continues to run. The whole mechanical feeder rests on the feedboard of the press and does not require nearly as much room as the pile feeder. When the sheets are placed on the feeder, they are rolled in much the same manner as for hand feeding on a slanting board above the actual feeding mechanism. These rolled-out sheets are then carried to the feeding devices by means of a wooden cylinder and heavy canvas tapes. Here the sheets are further rolled and separated by two large combing wheels. These same wheels also bring the sheets forward one at a time to the forwarding wheel which starts them over the slanting stationary sticks on their way to the guides. The sheet is controlled by small wheels and slowdown devices. It is positioned gently to the bottom guides and pulled to the side guide. This machine also has safety devices. Its only disadvantage is that, if there is no margin in which to put the combers when previously printed sheets are to be run, the ink on the sheets may smear.

On most flatbed presses the printed sheets are taken from the cylinder, carried forward over a series of tapes or by a chain conveyor, and placed on the delivery pile. The proper spacing of the feeding and delivery parts is important.

The grippers are also important in the delivery mechanism. Their proper location is the first step in obtaining the ideal arrangement of feeding and delivery parts. If the grippers are spaced evenly across the cylinder, it will be possible for the two bottom guides to be placed between any two grippers, and the various sheet sizes may be handled without moving the grippers or other parts.

For the older presses we next consider the sheet lifters or shooflies. The purpose of the shooflies is to lift the front edge of the printed sheet just as the grippers release it. Shooflies should be spaced about one-fourth inch from the grippers on the side of each gripper toward the center of the cylinder. This allows room for the bottom guides to clear both grippers and shooflies and insures that two shooflies will be directly in the center of the press. This is necessary while work-and-turn forms are being printed because they are sometimes slit on the backup. Any extra sheet lifters can be placed on the extreme ends of the rod and used when needed. The rod holding the sheet lifters can be removed by being forced toward the gear side of the press, freed at the center bearing which is merely a spring, and lifted free of the cylinder.

To set the sheet lifters or shooflies, the setscrews holding them to the rod are loosened, the sheet lifters are spaced to the grippers, and one of them is tightened on the rod. The tight sheet lifter is then lifted just enough to take up whatever play there may be in the rod and the next shoofly tightened on the packing. In the same way, the remaining sheet lifters may then be held to the packing and carefully tightened, the first one set being watched carefully to see that it does not rise away from the packing. If this does occur, the screw should be loosened immediately and reset so that the others are not disturbed.

After they are set, the shooflies should rise about $\frac{1}{4}$ or $\frac{5}{16}$ of an inch from the packing as the edge of the cylinder reaches the point of the strippers. To achieve this, the setscrew in the casting in the feeder end of the rod is loosened and the rod and all shooflies moved so that the tips of the sheet lifters will be closer to or farther from the packing, as needed. If this adjustment is necessary, the sheet lifters must be reset to the packing before the amount of lift is checked. A high sheet lifter will strike the form and will do serious damage if the press is backed excessively.

The stripper fingers are fastened to a rod which runs across the press and is just in front of the rear tape pulley wheel. The purpose of the stripper is to lift the sheet from the packing after the shooflies have raised it slightly. The pressman should set the strippers as follows: Loosen all setscrews on the strippers and place one beside each sheet lifter on the side toward the center of the press, just clearing the sheet lifter; allow the strippers to rest on the tape pulley shaft unless this shaft is badly bent, and tighten the setscrews; then loosen the setscrew in the stripper lever which is located inside the frame on the stripper rod at the gear side of the press, raise the stripper points so that they just clear the packing, and tighten the setscrew in the lever.

The sheet next moves on to the tapes which carry it forward to the delivery board. These tape pulleys should line up with the grippers on the cylinder. The tapes should be taut but not taut enough to spring the pulley shaft. They may be sewn or fastened with metallic fasteners which are applied with pliers. The full number of tapes should be carried on the machine to avoid unnecessary work when larger sheets are run.

The shooflies, stripper fingers, and tape delivery have all been eliminated on the newer chain-delivery Miehle presses which keep the sheet under positive control from the impression cylinder to the delivery pile.

Two delivery methods may be employed on the Miehle presses. The first is the face-up slide delivery, where the sheet is delivered to the delivery pile face up. The other is the fly delivery which delivers the sheet in a face-down position.

If the press to be run has a face-up slide delivery, the sheet is carried forward by the tapes or chain conveyor to the delivery pile. At the forward end of the press are the sheet stop fingers. These fingers stop the motion of the sheet as it is delivered from the tapes or chain conveyor. The front edge of the sheet should come up against the sheet stop fingers smoothly and without jamming. Adjustments can be made to achieve this. In most cases there are cam adjustments but in some cases there are tape speed adjustments.

The slide delivery may be converted on some of the older flatbed presses so as to place the sheets face down on the delivery pile. This method is known as the fly delivery.

The chain delivery is a conveyor with three delivery gripper bars, attached to endless chains traveling at a constant speed, which take the sheets directly from the cylinder grippers, carry them over vacuum slowdown wheels that retard their speed, and drop them gently on the pile. All of our newer Miehle flatbed presses have this chain delivery.

The automatic delivery system is actually an extended delivery with automatic lowering device. This device was used in 1897 by a printer in New York City who was running heavy stock and found that the stock piled on his delivery board too rapidly. It occurred to him to make some sort of extended delivery with a lowering device. A mechanism was devised which consisted of a wooden frame which would lower itself automatically. The delivery was extended far enough to bring the printed sheets out into the pile. This was a crude affair, but was the forerunner of the modern extended delivery. By 1910 all manufacturers of printing machinery had incorporated this feature in their presses.

This invention is a great boon to pressmen. Anyone who has lifted stacks of sheets 38 by 48 inches from the delivery board can readily understand this. The automatic delivery also has greatly improved the printed work. Much of the offset has been eliminated. Although this delivery device requires more floorspace, the saving in paper which was spoiled by the old method of handling and in manual labor is well worth the extra space required.

The speed with which the pile is automatically lowered is controlled to suit the various thicknesses of stocks. This adjustment consists of a simple ratchet and pawl. There is also a handwheel by which the pile may be operated manually to raise or lower it. The entire operation requires only a few minutes, and the only care needed is to oil the few moving parts.

The jogger blades, with adjustable supports, stack the printed sheets evenly onto the delivery pile. The front part of the sheet rests against stationary, long steel fingers. The blades open and close automatically with each impression and the sheet falls from the tapes or chain conveyor to the delivery pile when the blades are in their open position. To adjust the jogger blades, run a test sheet through the press to the delivery pile platform, and set the blades when they are in the closed position; that is, when the press bed is at front center.

Mention should be made here of a few miscellaneous delivery parts. Just beneath the front edge of the feedboard are several small thin wheels, each of which has a pointed outside surface. These are known as star wheels and are so positioned as to prevent the back edge of any heavy stock from rubbing on the underside of the feedboard on delivery from the cylinder.

Driving wheels are provided to keep the sheets traveling straight from the cylinder on delivery on all flatbed presses other than the chain-delivery Miehles. One set rides on the cylinder packing and is secured to the guide rod. These must always be set lightly to the sheet and clear of the grippers and shooflies. Another set rides directly on the tape pulleys. These should always be used when there is a margin which they can run.

Most of the larger presses are also equipped with a slitting attachment which slits the sheets in the center after they are printed. This is sometimes done on work-and-turn forms.

QUESTIONS FOR STUDY AND DISCUSSION

1. When was the first successful feeder developed?
2. Discuss the advantages of the pile feeder.
3. Discuss the stream feeder, its operation and advantages.
4. What is the purpose of the sheet lifters or shooflies? How should they be spaced?
5. Discuss the correct setting of the shooflies.
6. Where are the stripper fingers located? What is their purpose? How should they be set?
7. How should the tape pulleys be adjusted?
8. Discuss the faceup slide delivery.
9. Describe the facedown fly delivery.
10. What is meant by automatic delivery system?
11. Discuss the setting of the joggers.
12. What are star wheels? What is their function?
13. When is the slitting attachment used?

CHAPTER 29

Makeready for Cylinder Presses

SUBJECT OUTLINE

A. Packing cylinder.
B. Positioning sheet.
C. Cleaning press parts.
D. Positioning form on bed of press.
E. Locking chase on bed of press.

F. Positioning rollers.
G. Inking the press.
H. Pulling sheet to check position.
I. Marking out interlay.
J. Hanging overlay.

The first step in makeready of cylinder presses is the **packing of the cylinder**, which has been considered in an earlier chapter. A hard packing is used on jobs composed of plates or new type and a soft packing when the type is worn or when rush work is required. A soft packing generally requires very little makeready.

To remove the old packing, the front feed guides and feedboard should be raised and the press positioned with the packing reels on top and the grippers open. The reel holding the top sheet of the temporary packing is loosened and the press run around until the grippers show at the top of the cylinder. In this position the grippers are still open. The sheet lifters are raised by hand, the packing clamp lever opened with a pin wrench until the lever is free from the stud which holds it, and the old temporary packing removed.

The new temporary packing sheets are now applied and they should be pasted to each other and to the permanent packing, except on short runs. The packing clamps and sheet lifters are closed, the packing smoothed as the cylinder is run around until the reel comes into view, and the tail sheet reeled in. Allowance must be made for the thickness of the paper to be run on the job and one or two loose sheets of stock may be carried within the packing to be dropped when the overlay is hung.

173

The feedboard and drop guides are lowered ready to position the sheet. The **positioning of the sheet** on the feedboard depends on whether the job is to be automatically fed or hand-fed. If the sheet is to be automatically fed, it should be centered on the cylinder as nearly as possible, while for hand feeding it should be placed as conveniently as possible to the feeder side of the press. The grippers, shooflies, strippers, etc., should be centered on the sheet for either automatic or hand feeding.

The height of the feedboard and the adjustment of the guide tongues should be checked. The gripper bite should be roughly ¼ inch. The bite may be regulated by the adjustment of the drop guides and must be equal across the cylinder. When the sheet is in proper position on the feedboard, the distance from the edge of the sheet to the inside edge of the cylinder bearer is measured. This measurement will be useful when the form is placed on the bed of the press.

The pressman should **clean the press bed** and the cylinder bearers with a rag and Varsol. If a type form is to be run, the back of the form should be cleaned and wiped with a rag before it is placed on the bed of the press. The quoins also should be checked to see that they are tight before the form is lifted. If the form is on a patent base, the back of the base must be wiped clean before it is placed on the bed.

The **form is positioned on the bed** in the same manner whether it is a type form or mounted on a patent base. After it is placed on the bed, consideration must be given the deadline which can be gaged either by sight or with the deadline gage. The gripper edge of the form should be nearest the back or feeder end of the machine. If the margin to be carried on the gripper edge of the paper has not been specified it is best to center the form on the sheet. This is done by folding the sheet in the center the long way of the paper and placing the fold in the exact center of the form. The edge of the paper should extend ¼ inch beyond the deadline.

Wooden furniture is placed back of the form between the edge of the chase or base and the edge of the ink table. For small forms on large beds it is sometimes necessary to use metal spacing blocks instead of too much wooden furniture. If the margin to the side guide is known, it may be used as a gage to position the form sidewise. If it is not known, the sheet should be folded in the center the short way, centered on the form, and the measurement taken from the feedboard used between the edge of the sheet and the inside edge of the control side bed bearer. The chase is not locked sidewise on the bed for short runs except for close register work.

When **locking the chase on the bed** of the press, the pressman proceeds in the following manner: The quoins are loosened within the chase and the bed clamps tightened with the pin wrench. If the clamps are tightened too much, they will spring the chase. The procedure previously discussed for planing and carding type forms is now followed. The patent base is locked on, but before any impressions are pulled the plate catches are carefully checked. The procedure explained earlier for underlaying plates, either block mounted or mounted on patent bases, is followed.

The **positioning of the rollers** should be checked. The rollers are placed with the numbered end to the feeder side of the press. The form rollers are larger in diameter than the distributor rollers and therefore are easily distinguishable.

The **press is inked up** with a slow-drying ink. The ink is applied with an ink knife in an even line across the nearest angle roller to the front of the press and the press is run under power until the ink is properly distributed.

The next step is to **pull a sheet to check for position.** The margins specified are followed and the sheet checked to see that it is printing straight. When the sheet is held by the grippers, the gripper edge should be even with the folded edge of the packing. In order to maintain the proper gripper bite, it is sometimes necessary to twist the form slightly. After the image is straight on the printed sheet it is submitted for lineup and OK.

If a work-and-turn form is to be printed, a sheet must be backed up and printed on both sides to determine the register. To back up with accurate register by printing from the same guide, the following procedure is observed: A sheet is pulled and placed in position print side up on the feedboard and to the guides. A convenient register point is chosen near the side guide. This may be either the head or edge of a plate or print to be backed up.

A piece of paper about an inch wide and of the required length is now placed with one end against that part of the print to be used to register, the other end is extended beyond the side guide and held in place by a brad or the pointed end of the makeready knife. A mark has been cut through the paper at the point at the opposite side of the sheet which is to register on the backup. The sheet is turned over to the unprinted side and about ½-inch trim is cut off from the marked edge of the sheet margin.

The sheet is placed close to the guide, unprinted side up, and the edge of the narrow sheet held in place beyond the guide is matched with the cut through the sheet with which it is to register. The sheet is backed up and, if the register is accurate, it is then sent in for OK.

While the pressman is waiting for the return of the position sheet OK, a sheet is pulled for marking out the underlay. In the previous discussion on the interlay we learned that by this method plates are brought into proper contact with the rollers, much overlay is eliminated, and makeready is partially completed while waiting for the return of the lineup or OK sheet. To identify the pages, they are numbered on the sheet which is then ready to be marked out.

Two methods of marking out sheets are recommended. An extra sheet of the stock to be marked may be carried under the plate, removed, and replaced with the spotted-up underlay. Or spots which have been held to the marked-out sheet by small daubs of paste can be removed and pasted in proper position to the back of the plates. When this method is used, no sheets are removed from under the plate, unless the impression is too heavy. The marks from the back of the marked-out sheet are transferred to its face by placing a sheet of carbon paper face up under the sheet while marking out the back.

Only the general low areas in the impression should be marked out, no marks that are too small should be used, and the sheet should be marked out for folio only. Small patches on patent-base-mounted plates might sink in the plate lock channels and have no effect on the makeready. When in doubt as to whether or not a mark is needed, omit it. High places on impression or highlights on halftones should be reduced. Marking out for underlay differs from marking out for overlay in that the marks are not carried just to the edge of the low places but are kept a little inside of the area to allow for any bearing off or bending of the plate. Experience teaches how much allowance to make for this. The plates can now be underlaid and the register moves made at the same time.

The next step is hanging the overlay. Since we have already studied the overlay, only a brief review is necessary. The printed sheet is stabbed while it is still retained on the cylinder by the grippers, marked into sections if its size requires it, cut into sections, and the gripper edge trimmed to allow for hanging in the packing. All low places should be considered in marking out either for folio or tissue and heavy impression reduced by cutting out or scraping.

As little paste as possible should be used in spotting up to avoid wrinkling and making the print lumpy. If one overlay sheet will suffice, the low places on the face may be considered on this sheet also. The dog ears should be trimmed, the makeready hung, and a sheet of equal thickness removed from the packing if necessary. A second overlay should be hung if needed and the makeready is complete.

QUESTIONS FOR STUDY AND DISCUSSION

1. Discuss the removal of old packings and the process of placing new ones.

2. How is the sheet placed to position it for automatic feeding? For hand feeding?

3. What precautions should be taken to clean the bed of the press?

4. Describe the process of positioning the form on the bed of the press.

5. What procedure is followed by the pressman when locking the chase on the bed of the press?

6. What check should be made of the rollers?

7. What is the best method of inking up the press?

8. How is the sheet checked for position?

9. Discuss the process of backing up a work-and-turn form for accurate register.

10. What two methods of marking out sheets for underlay are recommended?

11. What areas should be marked out for underlay?

12. Describe the process of hanging the overlay.

CHAPTER 30

The Care and Operation of Cylinder Presses

SUBJECT OUTLINE

A. Care of the press:
  1. Oiling.
  2. Cleaning:
     a. Frame.
     b. Bearers.
     c. Zinc sheet.
     d. Belts.
     e. Electric motor.
  3. Replacing or repairing broken or worn parts.
  4. Adjusting.
  5. Setting the fountain.
  6. Placing the guide mark.
B. The press run:
  1. Placing the piled stock.
  2. Feeding the sheets:
     a. Push feeding.
     b. Draw feeding.
  3. Running the job.
  4. Inspecting for color.
  5. Conditions to watch carefully during press run.

Good pressmen are concerned constantly with the **care of the press**. All moving parts should be **oiled** regularly each morning or before starting a job and sometimes in the middle of the day on long runs. A careful study of the location of all oilholes should be made by the apprentice while the press is standing and while it is running. A thorough inspection of the working parts should be made while the pressman is oiling the press.

It is advisable to start the work of oiling at the same location on the press every time so that a regular procedure is established and no oilholes overlooked. The press should be adjusted so that the bed is at front center with the grippers at the top of the cylinder and the work of oiling started on the feeder side. It is very important to oil the gripper shaft and the bed tracks but not the leather cups on the air plungers. The press is readjusted so that the bed is to the back position and the bed tracks on the front end of the machine oiled. All holes under the ink table are oiled at this time. An oilhole may be a hole drilled in a casting or a well filled with waste. Copper tubing may lead to oilholes in hard-to-reach places.

Several means of supplying oil are used for the larger mechanisms which require a greater amount. One of these methods is the use of oilcups with spring-hinged covers. These cups are filled with waste to retain the oil and the waste should be removed occasionally to see that the oil is properly feeding to the parts. The waste within the cups needs to be changed at regular intervals.

Another means of supplying oil is provided by oilcups with glass sides and brass tops and bottoms. These cups may be shut off when not in use by an adjustment at the top which also regulates the flow of oil. This adjustment is turned clockwise to decrease the flow of oil. These cups are generally set so that one drop of oil will pass from them every 13 or 14 seconds. Some mechanisms may require a faster flow of oil.

Some of the presses have still another means of supplying oil. This consists of gravity-feed oilcups made almost entirely of a glasslike substance. The flow of oil from these cups cannot be regulated. They are filled by removing them from the press, turning them upside down, depressing the spring, and filling to capacity. The press should never be oiled while it is in motion if damage to the machine and injury to the pressman are to be avoided. However, modern presses are equipped with automatic pumps which supply oil to critical areas.

The press should be **kept clean** and all oil, ink, and dust wiped from the **frame** of the press at least once a week with a rag and Varsol followed by wiping with a clean rag. A clean press means better work and fewer inconveniences to the pressman. The bed and cylinder **bearers** should be wiped before every job and twice a day on long runs.

All presses in this Office have a **zinc sheet** for protection between the frame of the press and the floor which should be mopped every morning after the press has been oiled. The mop must never be used while the press is in motion because it can be caught in the bed motion of the press and cause serious damage.

The **belts** on the cylinder press must be wiped with a rag at least once a week to remove all oil, dust, and ink film. Older machines are equipped with leather belts which should be treated with belt dressing or neat's-foot oil at least once a month. Later machines have composition rubber belts which require only occasional inspection. When new belts are required, they are installed by the Machine Section.

The electric motor requires little attention except to be kept free of oil and dirt. Any troubles with the electricity such as arcing or sparking of the motor should be reported to the Electrical Section. All electrical repairs, however slight, are made by that section.

Any loose parts found on the floor or sections of the press should be traced. All broken or worn parts should be replaced or repaired immediately. Sometimes repairs are made to allow the press run to be completed and the actual replacement of parts is made on completion of the run.

The following adjustments may be made by the pressman and apprentice: grippers, stripper fingers, shooflies, fly cam or crank, all delivery adjustments, moving the cylinder ahead, and all simple adjustments. All major adjustments should be made only by a competent machinist: raising and lowering the cylinder, setting the cylinder lifting springs, and adjusting the bed mechanism.

In the setting of the fountain, the pressman chooses the ink to fit the job and fills the fountain about half full. All skin is removed from the top of the ink before it is placed in the fountain. After a sheet is printed, it is attached just below the fountain keys. It may be fastened from a wire strung from one end of the fountain to the other. The sheet is folded lengthwise in the center and hung over this wire in its proper position. If the form has been centered on the press, the sheet is hung in the center of the fountain. If the form has been placed for hand feeding, the distance from the bearer to the edge of the sheet should be measured and used to hang the sheet below the fountain.

The fountain is first set at the center and worked equally to both ends. In regulating the fountain flow, the fountain should be turned with the crank on the right or gear side of the machine and the amount of ink fed from the fountain to the ductor roller noted. All adjustments should be started at the center of the fountain and the fountain screws turned until the desired flow of ink is achieved. A slightly heavier flow is allowed for parts of the printed form which require more ink. The ends of the fountain and form margins are allowed a very slight flow of ink. The fountain should be set so that when the job is running about seven nicks are carried on the fountain feed ratchet to allow proper ink compensation. All parts of the rollers which are not touching the form should be coated occasionally with cup grease or oil.

The guide mark must be placed on all work except letterheads. This may be either a small brad which is driven in the furniture to an equal height with the rest of the form, a slug of linotype which is held in place by a quoin, or markers used for patent bases. It is placed at the side of the form nearest the guide and from 4 to 6 inches away from the gripper edge of the sheet. It must be right on the edge of the sheet as it will be trimmed off later. The guide mark is very important in later stages of work in the bindery and must not be omitted.

The sheet for final OK may now be submitted to the foreman and when the OK is received by the pressman he is ready to proceed with the actual **press run**. The feedboard is wiped with a clean rag to avoid damage to the paper. A lift of the stock to be fed, usually about 250 sheets or half a ream, is placed on the board. The stock is grasped at each edge and the sheets gradually rolled out toward the gripper edge. The edge to be fed to the gripper or drop guide will be inclined from the pile toward the guides. Now **the piled stock is placed** so that the edge of the top sheet to be fed is from 8 to 10 inches away from the drop guides. The edge to be fed to the side guide should be placed from 1 to 1½ inches away from the side guide to be used. Either guide may be used while feeding the cylinder machine.

Feeding to the far guide or the guide on the gear side of the press is known as push feeding. Feeding to the near guide is known as draw feeding. **Push feeding** is done in the following manner: Generally glycerine is used on the fingers of both hands by most feeders. The sheet is grasped in the upper right corner with the thumb and fingers of the right hand and flipped slightly to allow air to come between the sheets and separate the sheet to be fed from the rest of the pile. The sheet is guided to the bottom guides with the left hand and pushed gently to the side guide. Each job should be treated as a close register job and all sheets fed perfectly to the guides.

In **draw feeding** to the near guide, the sheet is started on its journey and fed to the bottom guides in the same manner as for push feeding. Whereas in push feeding the sheet is pushed to the guideline, in draw feeding it is drawn lightly to the side guide by using the tips of the fingers of the left hand. After skill in feeding has been acquired, it may be done with both hands resting on the feedboard. The best feeding is done in perfect rhythm with the movement of the guides, raising the hands as little as possible.

The pressman may now proceed with **running the job**. From 15 to 20 sheets are run and the last sheet examined for color or workups. The fountain is then reset from the center to the ends as required. During the run of the first two or three hundred, frequent **inspection for color** should be made. After the proper color is obtained, a sheet should be saved by which to match color frequently during the rest of the run. The ink in the fountain must not be allowed to get too low as this will produce a gray or oily color on the sheet.

During the press run, the pressman must always **watch carefully** for misregister, workups, pullouts, offset on the delivered sheet, slurs, wrinkles, and any changes that may occur in the makeready. When the press is left standing for a short period of time during the press run, the form vibrator rollers should be raised so as to clear the form rollers. This automatically releases the form rollers from contact with the ink table. If the press is left standing for a long period of time, the distributor rollers should be raised to their upper sockets which clears them of the vibrators and the ink plate. The press should be positioned so that the ductor roller is free of the ink plate and fountain. A little practice and experience will enable the apprentice to stop the machine in any desired position. The power should be shut off before the brake is applied. The printing press must not be backed excessively.

QUESTIONS FOR STUDY AND DISCUSSION

1. How frequently should the moving parts of the press be oiled?

2. Describe the operation of oiling the press.

3. What different means of supplying oil are used for larger presses?

4. By what means and how often should the frame of the press be cleaned? The zinc protective sheet? The belts?

5. Who makes all electrical repairs?

6. Which press adjustments may be made by the pressman or apprentice? Which should be made by the machinist?

7. Describe the setting of the ink fountain.

8. How is the ink flow regulated?

9. What is the guide mark? Why is it important?

10. How is the stock piled preparatory to feeding the press?

11. Discuss the process known as push feeding; and also that known as draw feeding.

12. What precaution is taken to insure even coloring of the ink throughout the job?

13. Name some of the conditions for which the pressman should be on the alert during the press run.

CHAPTER 31

The Adjustment of Kluge Feeders

SUBJECT OUTLINE

A. To print on various sizes and kinds of stock.

B. To prepare for makeready:
1. Run delivery arm forward.
2. Swing feeder magazine back.
3. Draw back delivery arm.
4. Lock the feeder head:
    a. Turn press forward.
    b. Pull back forward connecting rod.
    c. Release feeding arm lock lever.
    d. Raise feeding arm.
5. Makeready suggestions.

C. Set feeder for press run:
1. Position sheet holder tongue.
2. Attach side guide.
3. Set the feeder arm.
4. Set suction release valve:
    a. Rough setting.
    b. Micrometer adjustment.

D. Set the delivery arm:
1. Position suckers over platen.
2. Set the delivery suckers:
    a. For lightweight stock.
    b. For heavier stock.
    c. Coated or glazed paper.

E. Adjust the feeding magazine:
1. Mark the unprinted sheet.
2. Close the magazine.
3. Set the magazine guides.

F. To load the feeding magazine.

G. To provide the blast to separate the sheets.

H. To run the feeder.

I. To set the jogger:
1. Set guides.
2. Adjust jogger table.

J. Things to remember while operating the Kluge feeder.

This chapter deals with the adjustment of some of the parts of the Kluge automatic feeder. These adjustments are simple and they make it possible to run jobs ranging from the minimum to the maximum size that the press will print on various kinds of stock of any thickness from onionskin to eight-ply cardboard. Aluminum tips are used on the feeding arm for lightweight stocks and rubber feeding tips for heavyweight cardboard.

Makeready for the automatic feeder is the same as for hand feeding except that the patented Kluge side guide must be applied to the platen and the Kluge sheetholder tongue must be used. To prepare for makeready, the press is turned either by hand or under power until the delivery arm is run to its farthest forward position with the delivery suckers over the tympan.

The feeder magazine then is swung back until it is stopped by a safety device on the shaft on which the magazine hinges. The handle of the locking lever is raised to release the magazine. It is located on the press frame on the left or flywheel side of the press, directly under the left side of the feeder magazine. This releases it from the lug on the magazine frame.

The next step is to draw back the delivery arm. The pressman stands directly in front of the platen and with his left hand grasps the delivery arm near that part which is known as the swing joint. The arm is pulled back to the extreme end of the slide on which it operates, the nut on the swing-up joint is loosened, the arm swung to the vertical position, and the nut tightened with a $\frac{3}{8}$-inch open-end wrench.

The feeder head mounted on a shaft extending from the press frame at the right side of the press is locked. The press is turned forward until the lever on the other side of the shaft supporting the head comes in contact with, or opposite to, the stud on the inside edge of the eccentric. The groove in the lever must engage the eccentric stud.

The pressman grasps the forward connecting rod which actuates the eccentric, pulls back sharply, and at the same time presses down on the eccentric locking lever. This forces the stud in the eccentric in the locked position. The feeding arm lock lever just outside of the head eccentric is released and pulled toward the operator. At the same time the feeding arm is raised by grasping it just above the crossbar and pulling it toward the pressman until it comes to rest directly over the disk of the press. It is retained in this position by a stud located on the forward connecting rod.

Locking the head is one precaution which must be observed in order to prevent damage if it is operated during makeready. The head should be locked before the feeder arm is raised.

A few suggestions should be followed before the pressman proceeds with the makeready. The forms to be printed should be centered in the platen from right to left for best feeding results. When small sheets are run, the bottom guides should be located not more than 21 picas from the lower edge of the platen. The feeder can be adjusted to accommodate other locations, but best results are achieved if these general rules are followed. The lower gage pins should be positioned midway between the edge of the sheet and the center tongue. With these exceptions, the normal platen makeready procedure may be followed.

When the makeready is completed, the Kluge feeder may be set for the press run. The **sheet-holder tongue** attached to a clamp located in the center of the gripper bar must be positioned. Sheet-holder tongues come in six different lengths so one of the proper length must be chosen. Select one which will clear the edge of the sheet when the grippers are just half depressed. A tongue of this length will clear the lower edge of the sheet just before the side guide pushes the sheet to register. The only tool required to attach the sheet holder tongue is a screwdriver.

The next step is to attach the Kluge side guide which is held to a lug in the side guide rod. The grippers are depressed until they rest directly on the platen, the side guide positioned flat on the tympan in exact register, and the nut tightened. The side guide is provided with a screw which gives micrometer adjustment. This makes it possible for the guide to be moved in either direction to obtain exact register. Right-hand or left-hand guides may be used by changing the cam which operates the side-guide rod. This operating cam is just below the right-hand edge of the gripper bar.

The pressman is now ready to **set the feeder arm.** It is first lowered by returning it to its position above the packing. The spring-mounted latch which must be released to raise the feeding arm engage automatically when the arm is lowered. The eccentric lock is pushed up sharply to unlock the head and this releases the eccentric into operating position.

A sheet to be printed is placed against the bottom guides and the side guide and the press is run forward until the feeder-arm suction tips are $\frac{3}{8}$ inch above the lower guide edge of the sheet.. The outer suction tips should be spaced along the feeder bar midway between the bottom gages and the outside edges of the sheet to be printed. The inner suction tips are positioned equally between the two bottom gages. These suction tips are held to the crossbar of the feeding arm by spring tension and it requires no tools to move them. When a small sheet is being run and it is possible to use only two suction tips, the two outside tips are removed and the center ones used.

The **suction release valve** may be set with the suction tips positioned $\frac{3}{8}$ inch from the forward edge of the sheet to be printed. On the outside edge of the eccentric is a thumb nut which must be loosened. The trip stop lever on the inside edge of the eccentric should be raised as far as it will go. The suction release lever is pushed counterclockwise on the eccentric until the trip stop lever drops into position. The thumbscrew is tightened while the trip lever is in contact with the suction release lever. This is known as the **rough setting** of the suction release valve.

A final setting may be achieved by means of the screw located on the inside end of the trip lever. This is known as the final or **micrometer adjustment** and is made after the press is in actual operation.

To set the delivery arm, the clamp nut on the swing joint of the arm is loosened, the tube to which the suckers are attached is returned to its horizontal position, and the nut tightened. The lock at the back end of the slide is released and the delivery arm allowed to come forward to its operating position. The pressman then turns the press by hand until the **suckers are positioned over the platen** at their lowest point of travel.

The **delivery suckers** on the crossarm can then be **set** to a printed sheet. The two delivery suction tips are mounted on square, adjustable rods. A printed sheet is placed to the guides and the rods adjusted as required by using a ⅜-inch wrench to loosen the clamp nuts. The suction tips should be placed so as to strike in a blank area of the sheet to avoid a smeared or smudged appearance of the printed sheet.

The small tips which are used for the general run of **lightweight stock** require only ⅜-inch clear space. When it is not possible to have both suction tips horizontal or in line with the edge of the sheet, it is permissible to use them one forward of the other, but they should always be set as near to the rear edge of the sheet as possible. With the platen in its full open position, the tips should be adjusted so that they clear the sheet to be delivered by about 1/16 inch. At no time during the travel of the delivery arm should the tips brush the packing or the sheet.

When **heavier stock** such as cardboard is to be printed, the small suction tips should be replaced with the large bell-shaped tips. If there is not room for the tips to be placed in an unprinted area, a small piece of sandpaper with a hole in the center should be glued on the underside of the tips to allow sufficient suction to pick up the sheets.

It is sometimes necessary to use the large suction tips when printing **highly coated or glazed paper,** as the small ones will not deliver the sheet properly. On some jobs, it is possible to use only one suction tip, in which case the unused suction tube must be capped to prevent loss of suction.

The next step is to **adjust the feeding magazine.** A sheet of the stock to be printed is placed to the bottom guides halfway between the side guide and the register mark on the platen. Before the delivery is closed, the press is turned by hand to lower the feeding arm until the suction tips are close to the front edge of the sheet and the position of the left suction tip is **marked on the unprinted sheet.**

The press is turned by hand until the delivery arm is forward and positioned so that it will not interfere with the closing of the magazine. The magazine is swung into closed position so that the locking lever on the left-hand frame of the press engages in the locked position.

The two side stock guides are set to their extreme outward position by loosening the thumbscrews which hold them to the rod on the back of the feeding magazine. The sheet is now placed marked side up in the magazine on the elevator plate with the mark in the lower left-hand corner. The elevator crank on the right-hand side of the magazine is turned clockwise to raise the elevator plate to its full forward position and the elevator pawl lever which engages the crank ratchet is raised to hold it there.

The press is then moved until the feeder arm is in position at the magazine, the mark on the sheet is placed in register with the left suction tip, and the left stock guide moved to the left edge of the sheet. If the setting of the stock guide is correct, the sheet will feed to the platen slightly to the left of the final register position.

To load the feeding magazine, the elevator pawl lever which releases the ratchet is lowered and the elevator plate pulled to its rear position by means of the handle on the back of the plate. All stock should be jogged before it is placed in the magazine with the curl down if possible. After the magazine is fully loaded, the right stock guide is set close to the stock but does not bind it. The magazine should not be overloaded, and the uppermost sheet of the pile should not extend beyond the lowest comber mark about $1\frac{1}{2}$ inches from the upper edge of the base plate.

If the magazine is not completely filled, the elevator crank may be turned clockwise to raise the elevator advancing plate which in turn will lift the stock. The stock should be advanced to within $\frac{1}{4}$ inch of the suction pickup tips when they are at their rear position. The height of the pile is kept constant by an automatic device which is regulated by a small thumbscrew on the pile stop lever on a bar at the forward end of the magazine. A turn of the thumbscrew to the right keeps the stock lower within the magazine and a turn to the left raises it or holds it in a higher position. A space of $\frac{1}{4}$ inch between the top of the pile and the feeding tips should be maintained.

The blast required to separate the sheets to be fed is provided by three blast tubes or blower pipes on the forward end of the base plate. The main valve near the hinge on which the magazine swings away from the platen is connected directly to the blast line from the pump. Each blast tube also has an individual adjustment and the blast of air may be regulated as required. Enough blast should be used so that the upper sheets of the pile will float and become fully separated. This decreases the distance between the upper sheet in the pile and the suction tips.

A comber finger or separator spring is fastened to the forward end of each stock side guide. This spring should be set so that its pointed end is toward the center of the feeding magazine in order to separate more sheets as they are fed. A spring which extends through the hole with a center blower tube serves the same purpose.

To run the feeder, the feeder cut-off valve lever on the right side of the machine is turned to supply suction to the feeding and delivery tips. Suction is not supplied to the feeder until this lever is turned to the left even though the various feeder parts are in motion at all times when the press is running. The feeder may be shut off at any time by turning this same lever to the right.

While the press is feeding, the sheets should be released from the suction tips just as they contact the lower guides. If the sheets hit the lower guides too hard, the suction release micrometer screw on the feeding head should be turned clockwise until proper adjustment is obtained. The screw is turned counterclockwise to bring the sheet closer to the guides before it is released. A change in the speed of the press may require an adjustment of this screw.

The jogger may be set while the press is in operation. As the sheet is delivered from the packing by the delivery arm, the right and left guides are set to the edge of the sheet by loosening the thumbscrew under the base plate of the jogger. The position of the rear jogger plate may be changed by loosening the thumbscrew which holds the rod attached to the rear jogger plate.

The jogger table may be adjusted higher or lower by turning the handle at the left side of the jogger. The jogger table lowers automatically by means of a ratchet and pawl as sheets are placed upon it. In the center of the rear jogger plate is a small piece of metal mounted on a rod which controls the height of the pile in the jogger. This piece of metal is known as the feeler head, and no adjustment of it is required.

The Kluge press is equipped with a trip which throws the lever off automatically if the feeder misses a sheet, if the feeding magazine is empty, or if the operating cut-off valve is in its off position. When the impression trip lever is thrown to its off position, a small bell mounted on the press rings to attract the operator's attention.

Things to remember while operating the Kluge feeder: The sheets should be placed on the platen by the feeding arm about halfway between the side guide and the register mark. If this setting should change during the run, the position of the stock in the magazine may be changed by moving the side guides as required. It is not necessary to stop the press while this adjustment is made.

If more than one sheet is fed at a time, the stock pile is probably too high in the magazine. The stock should be lowered with the crank, and the thumbscrew which regulates the height of the pile turned to the right until proper feeding conditions are achieved. The sheets can be separated by resetting the comber springs on the edges of the guide and in the center hole of the magazine base. These comber springs brush the edges of each sheet as it is lifted from the pile by the suction tips and helps to separate it from the others.

These adjustments may seem very complicated and detailed at first but they will become very simple with experience.

QUESTIONS FOR STUDY AND DISCUSSION

1. What kinds of stock may be run on the Kluge feeder?
2. What adjustment on the feeding arm is made to accommodate light stock? Heavier stock?
3. To what position and by what means is the delivery arm placed in preparation for makeready?
4. How is the feeder magazine opened?
5. What method is used to draw back and tighten the delivery arm?
6. Where is the feeder head mounted?
7. Discuss the operation of locking the feeder head.
8. What suggestions should be followed before the pressman proceeds with makeready?
9. When the makeready is completed, what is the first step in setting the feeder for the press run?
10. How is the side guide attached?
11. Describe the setting of the feeder arm.
12. What procedure is followed to make a rough setting of the suction release valve?
13. By what means is a final setting of the suction release valve made possible?
14. How should the delivery be positioned to set the delivery arm?
15. What are the delivery suckers? How are they set?
16. What is the difference in the setting of the suction tips for light-weight stock, for heavier stock, and for highly coated or glazed stock?
17. What is the first step in the adjustment of the feeding magazine?
18. Describe the setting of the magazine guides.
19. What procedure is followed to load the feeding magazine?

20. How is the blast which separates the sheets provided?

21. How is the mechanism set to run the feeder?

22. Discuss the setting of the jogger.

23. What are some of the things to remember when the pressman is operating the Kluge feeder?

CHAPTER 32

The Mechanism of Miehle Vertical Presses

SUBJECT OUTLINE

A. Advantages.
B. Mechanism.
C. Frames:
    1. Main base.
    2. Way frame.
D. Installation.
E. Driving mechanism.
F. Stop cylinder:
    1. Simplifies impression.
    2. Achieves more accurate register.

G. Cylinder trip.
H. Outstanding features:
    1. Three points of support.
    2. Cylinder can be turned to any position.
    3. Simple washup.
    4. Combination guide and gripper bar.
    5. Efficient feeder.
    6. Pile tables.

Miehle vertical presses differ so greatly from most presses that this entire chapter is devoted to them. The vertical press appeared on the market about the latter part of the year 1921. It was the answer to a great need for an automatic job press to handle many classes of work easily. It met with immediate success and was a serious threat to platen presses because of its adaptability.

Many plants dispensed with platen presses entirely. Most of those in use in small shops were so old and worn that they had outlived their usefulness and many of them produced only the poorest class of work.

Feeders for platen presses were separate items of machinery. Some were of cheap construction and difficult to keep in good operating condition while others were used on old presses and were not giving satisfactory results. The inking mechanism was generally inadequate for all except light forms. The adjustment of the platen when changing from light to very heavy forms was difficult and impractical. Platen presses sometimes were not given the attention and care that all machinery should be given because they were low in price and were considered cheap machines by most pressmen.

It was only after improvements were made by manufacturers that the platen again found its place in the pressroom. Platen presses are now available as automatic units with the feeder and press suited to each other. They deliver a more rigid impression and are equipped with means of adjusting the impression as required. Great improvements have also been made in ink distribution. These features, together with higher speeds and better devices to maintain register, probably saved platen presses.

Some of the **advantages** of the Miehle vertical may be listed here. The first one introduced had a speed ranging from 2,000 to 3,600 impressions an hour and on later models the speed ranges from 3,000 to 5,000 impressions. The inking mechanism provides complete coverage for heavy forms. While the vertical uses only five interchangeable composition rollers, two of which are form rollers, two distributor rollers, and one fountain ductor roller, its inking ability is far above that of most presses of its size. Impression difficulties usually experienced on lightly constructed presses were overcome through the use of the small cylinder. Makeready time is reduced because the processes of changing forms, repacking the cylinder, and making necessary adjustments for the press run are easy.

The **mechanism** of the verticle press is simple. It occupies floor space of only 4 by 5 feet in its closed position and its height is 4 feet 6 inches. The bed, cylinder, and roller mechanism can be reached with ease when the feeder is swung away from the press. All press adjustments can be made with simple tools or no tools at all. Two pin wrenches of different sizes and a screwdriver are all the tools required. Other adjustable parts are equipped with handwheels or thumbscrews.

The press bed and cylinder operate against each other in the vertical position which keeps vibration at a minimum. The cylinder and the bed move up and down during the press run but they always move in opposite directions. These two parts are so well counterbalanced for a form of average weight that during their reciprocating motion there is only a small amount of vibration.

The vertical incorporates the general principles of both the platen and the cylinder press. The form is held in the bed in the same manner as on platen presses; that is, with the top part of the chase held against the bed by a clamp. The printing principle is similar to that on the cylinder press in that the sheet is fed to the top of the cylinder and the printed sheet removed from the same point.

The vertical press has only **two frames**. The first is the **main base** which houses the driving mechanisms and takes up all the driving strains. Attached to the base are the flywheel, motor pump, camshaft, crankshaft, and all other important driving units.

The second is the **way frame.** It is bolted firmly to the base and carries slides in which the press bed and cylinder mechanisms operate. It is designed to take up all the strain received while impression is being delivered. The bearing surface which supports the frame in which the cylinder is mounted is $26\frac{1}{2}$ inches long and $1\frac{1}{2}$ inches wide, which is large enough to furnish ample strength for any impression necessary. Far less pressure is required for printing than on platen presses and the larger cylinder presses because of the small diameter of the cylinder.

Most printing presses should be installed by a competent machinist or a factory representative because they must be leveled accurately. The vertical, however, has a three-point support by means of which all parts remain in alinement no matter what the condition of the floor may be when the press is installed or how much it may settle later. Although the press may still stay in alinement even when tilted to one side or the other, it cannot be operated if these conditions are carried to the extreme because the paper would slide out of place either in the delivery or in the feeder and the ink would run to one end of the fountain. Unnecessary wear at certain points will be caused if the press is run continuously while it is in an inclined position.

The **driving mechanism** which operates the counterbalanced bed and cylinder consists of a simple arrangement of racks and pinions which apply power to the bed-driving mechanism from a full-crank motion on the crankshaft of the press. The cylinder frame is then driven vertically by intermediate gears on each side of the way frame. The driving power is delivered by a 2-horsepower motor on the front end of the machine. This motor directly drives the pump and belt pulley. The flywheel is driven when the belt is tightened and it in turn drives the camshaft from which the various press accessories are operated. The feeder and delivery mechanisms, the ductor roller, and the valves which operate the various suction and blast devices are driven from the camshaft. Rapid operation of the press is possible by the counterbalancing of the bed and cylinder.

The vertical has a **stop cylinder** similar to those used on some of the earlier flatbed machines, a few of which probably are still in use. The stop cylinder was generally objectionable in the larger presses because of its size and the power required to stop and start it. However, the cylinder on the vertical press is small and very easy to stop and start.

The stop-cylinder mechanism has several other advantages. It greatly simplifies the mechanism required for impression as no special provision is needed to move the cylinder to and from the bed for the return stroke. The cylinder is held in a stationary position on the return stroke and a depression in the cylinder allows the form to pass without damage.

Another advantage of the stop cylinder is that **more accurate register is achieved** by having both the sheet and cylinder at rest as the grippers close. The cylinder is stopped and started while at dead center. Vibration and shock to the working mechanisms are avoided by this method.

No manual means of tripping the cylinder during the press run is provided on the vertical press. The **cylinder is tripped** automatically by means of suction holes which must be covered by the sheet to be printed after it is in register. It was the aim of the manufacturer to make the press thoroughly durable. Easy means are provided to take up any lost motion due to wear. The principal bearings are equipped with brass bushings which prevent wear as much as possible. All cams are split and may be removed and replaced easily when wear does show up.

Miehle vertical presses possess certain **outstanding features** not found in ordinary presses. They rest on **three points of support** and so are kept in constant alinement regardless of floor conditions. This feature makes possible the installation of the vertical press by the average pressman without the aid of factory-trained mechanics.

Another important feature is the fact that **the cylinder can be turned to any position** independently of the press at any time. This is a convenience while makeready is being attached or packing is being changed.

Washup is extremely **simple**, as it is not necessary to remove any of the rollers. The form and distributor rollers are held in position by two racks which separate the composition rollers from the steel vibrator rollers when unlocked and lowered to their vertical position. The fountain may be swung away from the frame for rapid cleaning. The rollers may be removed from their socket by the removal of a simple retaining key when roller changes become necessary.

Another new feature of the vertical press is the **combination guide and gripper bar.** No adjustment is required for different-sized sheets or different thicknesses of paper so the form must be correctly positioned within the chase. Small register moves may be made by raising or lowering the chase in the bed by means of the press jacks. The gripper bar also acts as the tympan clamp and holds the front edge of the packing securely to the cylinder. The same side guide may be used for either right or left register. The only tool necessary to change the guide from right to left is a screwdriver.

The feeder is very efficient. Suction and blast are supplied by a pump on the front or delivery end of the machine. The paper is fed automatically and any paper within the press range can be handled with very little adjustment. Adjustment to the suction which carries the sheets to the press is seldom necessary, as various pickup shoes are used for different weights of paper. The air blast which separates the sheets to be fed is adjustable by the opening of a petcock at the base of the feeder.

Two pile tables on the press hold the paper to be printed and the printed sheets. Both are automatic and can be raised or lowered as required. The feeder pile table can be swung away from the press so that the cylinder, bed, and roller mechanism are made easily accessible. Automatic trips throw the press off if a sheet fails to get down to the front guide or if sheets pile up on the transfer table. Mechanical fingers deliver the sheet from the cylinder and no adjustment of these fingers is required regardless of the size or weight of stock to be printed. The delivery requires no special shoofly fingers, stripper fingers, or tapes such as are found on flatbed cylinder presses.

QUESTIONS FOR STUDY AND DISCUSSION

1. When did Miehle vertical presses first appear?
2. What is the speed range of these presses?
3. Describe in brief the mechanism of the vertical press.
4. What parts of the mechanism are housed in the main base?
5. Describe the way frame.
6. Why is the installation of the Miehle vertical comparatively simple?
7. How is the driving power delivered?
8. What advantages has the stop cylinder on Miehle verticals over other presses?
9. By what means may the cylinder be tripped during a press run?
10. Discuss some of the outstanding features of Miehle vertical presses.

CHAPTER 33

Printing Illustrations

SUBJECT OUTLINE

A. Three methods of printing pictures.
B. Wood cuts.
C. Line cuts or zinc etchings.
D. Zipatone.
E. Halftones:
    1. Screen.
    2. Varieties:
        a. Outline.
        b. Vignette.

        c. Combinations.
        d. One-way.
    3. Height.
    4. Overlay:
        a. Mechanical.
        b. Hand-cut.
        c. Corrective.
    5. Amount of ink.

The printing of illustrations is a very important phase of presswork, for without them printed matter would be very dull indeed. **Three methods of printing pictures** from metallic plates are intaglio, planographic, and letterpress. Intaglio printing includes photogravure, rotogravure, steelplate, and copperplate. Planographic printing includes lithography, offset, aquatone, and other similar processes. This discussion concerns letterpress printing and will be confined to the photomechanical processes and the use of wood and linoleum cuts.

Wood cuts are the oldest form of printed illustration. Evidence shows that they were used by the early Egyptians and Romans and that wood engraving was practiced in China as early as 1120 B.C. Although various kinds of wood were utilized, probably the most widely used was boxwood. It was the choice of most engravers because of its close grain and its ability to hold fine, clean, unbroken lines. The use of wood cuts continued until about A.D. 1890, when they were replaced generally by illustrations produced by modern processes. At the present time wood and linoleum cuts are produced as hobbies.

The wood engraver was a true artist and his work was exacting. He first planed and polished the block to be engraved until it was exactly type high. He then drew directly on the surface of the block a sketch of the drawing to be engraved and used engravers' tools to cut away nonprinting areas. The solids or lines left standing were then of the thickness required by the original sketch, and the nonprinting areas were made deep enough to prevent their filling with ink and printing when impression was applied. Wood cuts have given good results on all finishes and grades of paper and have been printed satisfactorily in several colors.

The photomechanical process of making plates for printing, including **line cuts or magnesium and zinc etchings**, will now be considered. The kind of engraving to be used is generally determined by the copy available. A picture composed of plain black lines is ideally suited for line etching. For this reason, pen-and-ink sketches, outline maps, ink signatures, comic strips, and similar illustrations lend themselves to this process. In printing color supplements such as the Sunday newspaper comics, the outline of the figures is usually reproduced in black and a separate plate made for each color.

Magnesium and zinc etchings or line cuts are the simplest, cheapest, and probably the most widely used means of reproducing engravings. The copy should be black, yellow, orange, red, or brown, as all these colors photograph well and produce satisfactory negatives. Blue and other colors which do not photograph so well should never be used in the preparation of copy.

Special patterns or screen effects on certain portions of the line etchings are produced by the artist pasting Zipatone over portions of the copy he wants shaded. This Zipatone is manufactured with an adhesive on one side and can be cut to any shape and pasted directly on the artwork. It comes in many attractive designs and tone values ranging from a fine highlight dot to almost a solid. Coarse tones are used on engravings that print on newspaper or coarse papers and fine screens on engravings that print on smoother stock. Any number of the various designs and screen tones can be used on the same cut. This process is generally used in newspaper work or the cheaper illustrated booklets. The character of the stock on which the job is to be printed materially influences the preparation of the cut.

Pictures with shaded portions that blend into one another and with no well-developed black-and-white areas should be reproduced by **halftone** plates because halftones reproduce all the intermediate gradations of color from black to white, including the in-between colors or halftones. They may be used to reproduce copy of any kind, including photographs, wash drawings, and oil paintings. The halftone process should also be used for illustrations which are printed in many colors.

The **screen** used in the camera while the copy is being photographed makes this reproduction possible. It consists of two glass plates engraved with fine parallel lines and cemented together so that the lines cross each other at right angles to form a mesh or screen which may vary from 50 to 175 or more parallel lines to the inch depending on the paper to be used. Newsprint and offset require halftones with 50 to 85 line screen; antique stock, 60 to 100; machine finish and sized and supercalendered, 85 to 120; English finish, 100 to 133; coated book papers, 120 to 150; and double-coated and enameled book papers, 133 to 175. About 45 different operations are required to produce a single-color halftone plate.

Many **varieties** of effects are possible in halftone plates. For example, the **outline** halftone is an illustration in which the background has been entirely cut from the picture and the reproduction is printed in the exact shape of the original. The **vignette** halftone has a background which gradually fades away until it becomes lost with the surface of the paper. **Combinations** of linecut and halftone plates may be produced in the one engraving. **One-way** halftones have all the screening lines running in one direction to give an effect similar to the old wood cut.

It is necessary for the pressman to give more care to the printing of illustrations than to the average job. It is very important that the cuts be brought exactly to type **height**, except for large, solid areas which must be made slightly more than type high because of the extra pressure required to print them. This extra pressure must be divided between the plates and the packing. Vignette cuts must be kept slightly less than type high so that the edges may be made ready properly. This careful handling of cuts is necessary in order that the inking rollers will ink all portions of the cut. It is also essential to use the best rollers available and to see that they are properly set. The reproduction of halftones requires special ink for satisfactory results.

After the form has been properly prepared by underlaying, an **overlay** should be applied in the packing. On very fine halftone work it is important that extreme care be given when marking out the illustrations. Pull an impression on coated stock with a light impression and light ink coverage. This will show the weak areas which can be marked out by using a carbon sheet mounted on a cardboard. The halftones on the printed side of the sheet are marked out for tissue and the carbon paper under the sheet transfers the marks to the back. Confine the marks to a maximum of three for any given area. The solids, middletones, and highlights within the halftone are not considered in the process of marking out as the marks are made to provide just enough pressure to make all dots, regardless of their size, print as complete circles. Tissue only should be used because paper of greater thickness may bear off.

Halftone solids require more pressure than the highlights. This pressure can be applied by using mechanical or hand-cut overlays. The **mechanical** overlay used in the Government Printing Office is the 3M process and the procedure for its use will now be discussed.

The spotsheet or overlay with the tissue patches should be applied before the 3M overlay so that the weak portions of the halftones can be properly marked out. It is much more difficult to properly mark out and level the halftones if the 3M is put on first. After leveling the form, cut the 3M overlay sheet off the roll to the correct size. The sheet is then printed with regular black ink, somewhat darker than the amount needed to run the job and with an extra sheet of impression. Stop the printed 3M sheet in the grippers and stab it like the regular spot sheet. The printed sheet is placed in the dry-process machine and held by clamps. Remove the exposed makeready sheet and paste it to a manila in the cylinder packing just under the two top manilas. Be very careful to place it accurately on the stab marks. A special 3M paste is provided to hold it in place.

For light forms with short runs on the lower quality work, **hand-cut** overlays called skellies are frequently used. This is done by printing on a sheet of lightweight coated or machine-finish stock, with enough pressure and ink to obtain a good print. Then cut at the edge of the halftone print or no more than one point in from the outer edge. Cut out the highlights and paste the dark portion on the spot sheet that has been marked out and filled in to level the form. Hang this completed overlay in the packing as explained earlier.

The **amount of ink** needed for jobs containing halftones must be controlled at all times to prevent the screen in the halftones from filling up and producing a poor print.

QUESTIONS FOR STUDY AND DISCUSSION

1. Name three general methods by which pictures may be printed from metallic plates.

2. What is the oldest form of printed illustration?

3. Describe the work of engraving a wood cut.

4. For what kind of illustrations are line cuts or zinc etchings specially suitable?

5. What pictures are suitable for reproduction by the halftone process?

6. What effect does the screen used in the camera have on the kind of halftone produced?

7. Describe an outline halftone, a vignette halftone, a combination cut, a one-way halftone.

8. How is the accurate height of the cut obtained?

9. Why is it necessary to have careful control of the flow of ink when halftones are being printed?

10. Describe the procedure for using the 3M overlay.

CHAPTER 34

Web Presses

This chapter covers in some detail the operations of the web presses in the Government Printing Office. Those aspiring to achieve the status of web head pressman need not only the background of flatbed work but extensive training on the more complicated machinery of the web unit. Experience can be supplemented by the knowledge imparted by other men in the unit. The following pages contain a résumé of information compiled by web pressmen.

The second word a man hears after the word "web," which incidentally is the sheet of paper in the press, is the word compensate or compensator. Since the web is theoretically an endless sheet, controls to guide it into the folder and keep the print in constant position are essential. First, a compensator is a movable idler roller over which the sheet passes and it lengthens or shortens the distance a sheet must travel. A straight line is the shortest distance between two points. Therefore, a movable compensator will give control by holding back the print or letting it go forward as the case may be. The next step is to learn how and when to make adjustments.

The pin edge should always be the guide. For instance, on 5980, the pressman knows that "A" press is the outside form and prints first, and "B," the inside, prints second; therefore, by moving the compensator he is able to register "A" with "B" after checking the print to see whether "A" must move toward the pins or away from the pins.

This same principle holds true for all compensation whether main or individual.

The exception is rotary web press No. 1. This postal-card press is the oldest press in the office and the pressman must be guided by the print or cut marks because there are no pinholes to serve as a guide.

Bars in the folders are used for alinement of ribbons in the folder. Before making any further description, the following warning must be issued: Pressmen should not alter the angle setting of bars on Groups 56–54 or 57 as this must be done by a machinist with correct tools and instruments. Bars on Group 59 are not so critical but should not be moved indiscriminately. Arrows have been painted on these bars and

676361°—63——15

generally a clockwise movement will move the bar and ribbon toward the operator.

Main bars present a different problem in that they move the whole web before it enters the slitters. This bar corrects any lateral movement by the web due to paper difficulties, etc. A pressman can stand in front of the folder and watch his ribbons line up while moving the main bar. Individual bars line up the ribbons after the slitting operation. If the guide is checked before moving, some unnecessary movement can be eliminated. It must always be remembered that any bar movement will cause a change in the compensation and this adjustment will have to be made accordingly.

Idler rollers, free or driven, are rollers that support or guide the web. Some are compensators and others are fixed. It is possible to cock these rollers but adjustments should be made only by experienced men or machinists since they should be perfectly level. Group 59 has an adjustment on one side to cock the idler to line up head margins of "A" press with "B." It is not advisable to move these rollers unless absolutely necessary. Remember that any movement of the idler away from the level will cause the web to travel to the high side.

One adjustment in the folder that should be made with great care is that involving pinch rollers.

The new Record presses contain individual pinch roller control while all the other presses must be adjusted in a different manner. Generally speaking, adjustment should not be too tight since it will cause the web to pull tight and break. When the pressman sets the pinch over the cutting cylinders it must be tight enough to keep it from slipping. In other words, count the ribbons and put an equal number in the pinch, bring the roller in until the sheets are snug and become difficult to move. Then make an additional quarter turn which gives enough pressure to hold the ribbons firm.

When adjusting presses where the pinch rollers are part of a common shaft, care must be taken to bring both sides up even. The Group 56 presses have an adjustment on each end and one in the center, hence all three are set simultaneously.

The forwarding rollers on all presses should be set with a signature in place and sufficient pressure applied to hold the signature firmly and yet not too tight. Correct setting of the forwarding rollers is necessary to prevent jamming in the delivery or on the transfer, since this grips the signature firmly and forwards it into the delivery gripper. The signature should be advanced to the point where it is free of the jaw gripper and then adjustment made.

Placing and adjusting of guards and bands are important not only to performance but to the quality of work. Guards merely support the book as the collects and transfers are made. Caution should be used in moving the guards since they may interfere with some other part of the folder or rub against the cutting cylinder, etc. Movements to prevent smearing should be made only when adequate support of the sheet will be maintained.

Bands should be set against the collects snugly and evenly otherwise the lip of the book will be uneven. This operation is very delicate and, unless the operator is experienced, he should not move them. Extreme caution should be taken if it is necessary to make adjustments while the press is running. Books should be placed side by side as in 2/32's and comparison made to see if the band is causing the fold to be crooked. Again the pin is the guide. A tight band brings the fold nearer the pins while a loose band will drop it away and, if both bands are too loose, the books have a tendency to buckle on the folding edge.

Since the web press is a complex piece of machinery, the operator should train himself to recognize various danger signals. We shall discuss these various danger signals given by the press itself to help the operator forestall serious accidents. As noisy as the machinery is, the operator can train himself to recognize foreign noises. It is his responsibility to find or have determined what is causing this foreign noise. It may be a loose guard or a loose cam. At any rate, 95 percent of the time it is a prelude to trouble. Proper lubrication is one remedy and all pressmen should acquaint themselves with the oil and grease fittings. Regular inspection trips often reveal loose fittings or improper action. For instance, after the Cottrell presses were installed and running, a small pile of steel filings was noticed beneath a cam on a roller carriage. Inspection revealed that grease fittings had been obscured by the cam and the race was chewed up for lack of grease. If books suddenly start to fold crooked or the fold seems out of line, this indicates broken tucker blades or blades out of adjustment. If dropping collects begins, check the pins, for they may be broken. If the pin is broken off, then replace it immediately for this can lead to a jam. It is often possible for a pin to be broken off and yet appear to be working. This is especially true on the Group 56 presses, where pins break and stick in the rubber without ducking so that it gives the appearance of being whole. Also on these groups it is possible for a guard to work up and touch the tucker blade in the collecting cylinder, causing it to drop a collect or pull them off the pins. Examination of the product often reveals clues to the trouble. For instance, the cutting edge will reveal whether the cutting is clean or not. On the above groups, cutting rubbers are usually the culprits and should be changed. In any event, this is a machinist's job. It is also the machinist's responsibility to determine whether sharper knives are needed.

Other signs of trouble may manifest themselves through certain marks on the paper. Examples are nailheads working out of the cutting rubber and guards touching the sheet and causing a definite impression. If the web is continually breaking in the folder, check the pinch for if this is too hard, it will produce breaks in the ribbons. The next thing to examine will be the pinch rollers riding on the driven idlers. These should be set with even pressure, but rubber swells, so they should be checked. Next see if they are running true. If not, remove and place new ones on. The same holds true for the slitters. One difficulty with knives is that the successive grindings bring them well below the satisfactory diameter needed to slit properly. This is especially true in the delivery where the knife must fit deep enough into the slot to cut the book cleanly. When setting a slitter, bring the flat side of the slitter up to the side of the slot but free it enough to keep it from binding.

Whenever cutting rubbers are put in, the cylinders should be backed off and web removed while running the press to wear them in. After five minutes of this, bring the cylinders back to the mark slowly. If cylinders are not brought back to near the marks on the cylinders, relationship between pin heights on the transfer is affected and collects on the transfer may be lost. Pin height should not be more than ¼ inch on Group 56 and ⁵⁄₁₆ inch on Group 59.

There is one practice which should be stopped. It ruins more rollers than any other. This is the practice of throwing the cylinders open with the ink carriage closed to allow splices to pass through. The action of the cam throws the plate cylinder back against the form rollers and, if the edge of the type matter catches the impact, it will tear holes in the surface of the roller. Discretion should be used in opening and closing cylinders for splices.

This part shall deal with rollers, their care, setting, and printing characteristics. First, Group 59 has been converted to synthetic rubber rollers nearly 100 percent. These rollers should have a durometer reading of between 15 and 20 points of hardness as per present Government Printing Office specifications. Setting picture should be ¼ inch to ⅜ inch on the form and the same on the distributor. Whenever possible, pictures should be taken off the roller impression on the drum and on the form. Haphazard setting through use of a feeler does not give as accurate or satisfactory results.

When to change rollers or replace with new ones can be highly controversial. Here are a few guideposts for pressmen to follow when using the Ideal covered or composition rollers on rotary presses. Many times ink has been blamed where a roller has been at fault. A bad roller will not cover the type matter properly and will, in fact, produce a wiping action. If the typeface is examined closely, especially on boldface type, the character will appear to have the ink pushed to one side and the job appears to be light. Therefore, there will be a tendency to add ink, which will cause more streaking in the folder. Actually, what is taking place is that the ink has piled on the edge of the character and is being scraped off on the bars, idlers, or guards, and building up a deposit. The operator will clean and scrape three or four times a day or run a job light and dirty. Some men have mistaken roller trouble for makeready breakdown without examining the back of the sheet. Changing rollers are quite a chore but the benefits derived will more than repay your efforts. By examination of the roller itself after being washed up, determination of its usefulness by sight and feel can be made. A hard and glazed surface will indicate that the roller is "dead." Distributor rollers should be kept clean of dried ink deposits and checked for breaks or peeling. Most of these rollers have been converted to synthetic rubber and appropriate care should be given them. Dried ink or buildup on distributors has a tendency to break up after a period of time and will put dirt in the form. Ductor rollers are often the cause of putting dirt in the form when dried ink begins to break up. If a sleeve ductor is being used and is filling the form, the best remedy is removal and replacement. Care should be exercised in the setting of ductors to prevent them from striking the ball or drum too hard.

Packing web press cylinders should be done with care and preciseness. When packing hard-packing presses, pressmen should follow the prescribed packings. Experience has shown that deviation will cause packing creeps with all the resultant trouble. Makeup of these packings should follow a general pattern. Usually they are made up of five to six machine-finish sheets that have been cut to size. They should be boxed and laid out on a flat surface. Hold firm with one arm and lightly paste each sheet to the next. Then fold the whole unit with about one and one-eighth inch lip. It is advisable to use a straightedge when folding this lip for, unless extreme care is taken, a bow may result which will cause a bulge on one side of the cylinder when it is put in place and drawn up. Packings and top sheets should be pasted into place for security.

The other soft-packing presses utilize a blanket and patent drawsheet and are not too difficult to put on. The Cottrells require special tools and experience to repack. In all cases blankets and top sheets should pull square. Sometimes a blanket may stretch and bulge the back of the packing. This condition can be corrected by cutting the excess off the blanket.

Where cylinders contain a slit bar to reel in the packing, do not tighten reel with a deliberate, steady motion. Rather, when taking up slack on the reel, do it with the fingers, then rock it back and forth with the wrench. This movement will settle the top sheet in the reel and it will pull up smoother. Again when putting on a fresh packing or top sheet, it should not be pulled up too tightly as it may pull from clamps before paste has set.

Since all of our presses are perfectors, that is, print on both sides of the sheet, please note the different top sheets in use on the second cylinder. We use a material that will repel ink when impression is applied. This material is made up of tiny glass balls bonded to a common surface. Thus, by using this surface and an oil wiper, about 90 percent of offset on the back of the sheet can be avoided and buildup of ink on the packing can be prevented. It is possible for ink buildup to reach a stage where it batters the plate.

Starting with the smaller presses, we will endeavor to give a little more detail of each press group. The smallest book web press is the speech press, generally used to print speeches for Congressmen. This press prints signatures 6 by 9½ inches of 4, 8, 16, or 32 pages at speeds over 6,000 per hour. It is also equipped to paste and perforate with the fold of the signature.

The larger book web presses or magazine webs can produce two 32-page books folded to 6 by 9½ inches at a top speed of 6,500 per hour. Most of these presses are equipped with marking devices to count and separate the books at the press. Rolls of paper 9½, 19, 28½ or 38 inches in width can be used on this group.

Two magazine presses are equipped with stitchers. One has a stitcher and a paster, the remaining press is equipped with paster and perforator.

The Record presses can run signatures up to 64 pages at speeds in excess of 15,000 per hour. A booklet can be stitched or pasted and perforated on this press group. They have permanent packings so all makeready has to be done under the plates.

The makeready varies with the job. Most runs of less than 100,000 with few halftones and not A-1 quality can be made ready under the plates. A soft packing eliminates the need for much makeready. On the other hand, A-1 work and halftone jobs require leveling under the plates, a hard packing for the spot sheets, and in some instances a mechanical overlay. Start all halftones one sheet lighter under the plate than the rest of the form.

The type of stock will help determine the amount of makeready. Machine-finish paper and newsprint are very easy to print on and require underlays only. Most sulphite papers also fall into this category. Machine-coated and supercalendered papers that will contain cuts require a hard packing and normal makeready procedure. Any job calling for English-finish paper should run on a hard packing with an overlay.

Since paper is fed from a roll, web-press problems are vastly different from those of sheet-fed machines. Some paper rolls will not be cured evenly, resulting in a loose side, or become "baggy." This will affect your compensation and, if severe enough, the ribbon will begin to weave back and forth. Now this should not panic the pressman into thinking something has gone wrong with his press. Look at the web and see how it runs or hangs. One of the first remedies is to run with as little tension as possible. Second, on magazine presses take the roll off and turn it around. This will often clear up the trouble. Third, make sure press adjustments are normal. The last resort will be to report the situation to the desk. This is important since it can result in the recovery of lost time. The testing division will verify the defect in the paper and a latent-defect report is made out. Lost time will be charged against the stock. Bad splices, slime holes, etc., that are causing trouble should be recovered since this is bona fide evidence to be submitted to the company responsible. These improprieties, plus the roll, order, and property numbers should be turned over to the supervisors.

Examination of rolls before splicing can save many a web break. Sometimes glue from a wrapper will adhere to the ends and paste the succeeding wraps together. Foreign particles and damaged ends should be removed or marked so that portion can be run with caution.

The trainee must remember that web presses, as a rule, are custom made to include many bindery operations or other special operations. Many of the particulars referred to here would not apply to other web presses but the basic fundamentals would. Therefore, the mysteries of web presses can be simplified by the application of the principles described in this chapter.

QUESTIONS FOR STUDY AND DISCUSSION

1. What is a "web"?
2. Describe the movement of the compensator and its purpose.
3. In making folder adjustments, what is used as a guide point in the book?
4. Discuss the various danger signals given off by the press itself.
5. What two classes of packings are used on web presses?
6. What factors determine the value of web press production?

CHAPTER 35

Time Reporting

The presswork trainee will realize very soon that time reporting plays an important role in the pressroom. The Government Printing Office is equipped with a modern cost-accounting system, including electronic data processing. Through this medium, cost summaries of every job performed in the Office can be obtained. In addition, information is supplied which gives section and press performance.

One of the questions invariably asked by a new employee or trainee when discussing costs is, "Why does the Printing Office go to so much detail to determine costs when performing work for other agencies? Aren't we working for the same Government?"

The answer is simple. First, the production divisions of the Printing Office do not work from an appropriation. The ordering agencies pay the Printing Office for services rendered from agency appropriations. Therefore, it is just as important for the Office to know its costs so it can bill properly the agencies as it is for private printing concerns to determine their costs in order to compete in open markets. In addition, it is the desire of the Public Printer to give quality and service to the ordering agencies as economically as possible.

The trainee in the Letterpress Division must acquaint himself with the card system of reporting, since every operation he performs and every minute he works must be recorded.

There are three categories of cards:

1. Payroll card for the individual. This card is salmon in color and must be pulled from the rack at the beginning of the shift by the individual whose name and rate of pay are printed thereon and then deposited with the timekeeper.

2. Cost-distribution card. This card is white in color. The assignment of the individual determines the operation and class number to be used on the cost-distribution card. In essence, this card carries the labor charge for the employee assignment. For instance, a cylinder pressman assigned to Press 575 would file a white card with operation 190, class 2– which means he is tending a press as a pressman. The employee fills in the press number and group number and deposits this card with the timekeeper to whom he is assigned.

3. Machine-production card. This card is yellow in color. All operations and classes of work are recorded along with the jacket number, press number, and group number. As each operation and class is completed, it is charged out at the clock and a new card is stamped in for the next operation and class. Machine production in the pressroom falls into various classifications. The main classifications are:

a. Chargeable time or time that can be charged to a jacket. These operation numbers are within the 100 category and explain how the time is charged, whether it is makeready, running, or a direct charge to the jacket.

b. Nonchargeable time when the press is manned. This is a 200 operation with various classes to explain the reasons for delay.

c. Nonchargeable time where the press is unmanned. This is a 300 operation with various class numbers to explain why the press is idle.

Before proceeding further it should be explained that each trainee will be provided with a book titled, "Schedule of Operations and Classes of Work, Letterpress and Offset Divisions." This book contains all operations and classes of work that pertain to presswork operations. The trainee is encouraged to consult his supervisor, the timekeeper, or the press reviser at any time to clarify use of these operations and classes. The trainee must understand that these are general instructions and that detailed instructions will be received from the instructor, the timekeeper, or his supervisor. Operation and class numbers for production cards are placed on revises by the press revisers.

However, familiarity with operation and class numbers prevents expensive mistakes in recording. As a word of caution, the pressman or trainee should exercise care in filling out production cards since the cost of correcting each error fluctuates from $5 to $25.

These cards, through electronic data processing, also provide the foreman with a record of individual machine production. The new pressman or trainee has a tendency to follow certain unauthorized work standards usually set forth by the employees themselves. This is a misconception of production standards. Standards are set up for the purpose of estimating costs but these are based on an average performance of the press group. This can best be demonstrated by example:

Standard makeready time for a group of presses may be 3.5 hours on a class of work involving halftones. It stands to reason that a form with one halftone cut is going to take less time to make ready than a form with twelve. The form with twelve halftone cuts may take 5 or 6 hours, so in order to average the 3.5 hours over a period of time, many of the easier forms would have to be completed in less than

3 hours. There is a tendency on the part of some to charge close to the 3.5 hours on the easier forms and then when the hard ones come along their average deteriorates. The average for that group will then rise over a period of time to maybe 3.9 hours per form. Prices will then be based on this new figure; the vicious circle starts again and soon we would be priced out of business.

So, we find that it is important for the pressman and the trainee to make honest reports. The foreman receives daily, monthly, and annual reports providing him with a complete picture of individual press performance. Monthly responsibility report meetings are held by the comptroller in which your supervisors participate in cost discussions and cost analysis.

This method of reporting is not as complicated as it may appear at first. Many employees are prone to accept it as a necessary evil without realizing that it is a vital part of our job. It represents not only control of costs but provides a barometer by which all of us can measure our production and efficiency.

QUESTIONS FOR STUDY AND DISCUSSION

1. Why is it necessary for the GPO to maintain a modern accounting system?

2. What are the three categories of timecards with which the trainee must be familiar?

3. What are the principal sources of information regarding the time system?

4. Why is it important that errors be avoided?

5. What reports are furnished to the foreman by the comptroller through use of electronic data processing and what use can be made of them in production?

CHAPTER 36

Modernization

There have been many new developments in the letterpress industry that have come about due to the rapid development of the offset method. The trainee will note that flatbed cylinder presses over the past 50 years have remained essentially the same design with improvements in the delivery and the feeders. The greater demand for printing calls for faster makeready and higher production speed.

Thus we find that sheet-fed rotary and the web-fed rotary are coming more into prominence. The widespread use of camera copy lends itself very well to the offset method of printing. It was along these lines that letterpress had to find a medium of production to compete favorably with the offset method. To remain in a competitive position, the "wrap-around" letterpress has been developed and has now entered the commercial field. The GPO, endeavoring to remain abreast of modern developments, has recently authorized the purchase of two of these presses.

Wrap-around utilizes the many advantages of offset imposition, using camera copy, repros, etc. Up to the point of burning in the plate, operations are the same as preparing for offset. The plate is "burned-in" by passing light through the negative to the sensitized surface of the plate. The plate is then removed to an etching machine and etched to a depth of 0.012 to 0.015 inch. The plate is then locked on the plate cylinder in the same manner as an offset plate. The inking system consists of a cylinder of similar size to the plate having a rubber blanket to receive the ink transfer from the inking rollers. The ink is then transferred to the plate in a one for one ratio. This provides a precision transfer of ink and eliminates possibility of "ghosting."

Fidelity of color throughout a run is one of its many advantages and the press has found increasing favor among color and label houses. The method of ink transfer is very important due to the shallow nature of the plate and the possibility of "bottoming" or printing of shallow areas on impression.

The process is basically letterpress and should not be confused with dry offset because there is no transfer of the image to a blanket. The plate image is transferred directly to the paper by pressure.

There are many materials from which to make wrap-around plates. Some of the more prominent are zinc alloys, dycril or photopolymer, copper, aluminum, and rubber. The unique feature about the process is that makeready as we know it is practically eliminated. The solidity of impression, the transfer of ink, and ease of plate imposition have created great interest in the wrap-around method.

Many authorities are of the opinion that it represents the only hope of survival for the letterpress as a major printing medium.

Recently, the GPO purchased a Heidelberg platen press that has found great favor among job printers throughout the United States. The press is unique and provides many advantages over the conventional platen.

The press provides a very solid impression. The sheet is gripped throughout the printing cycle by a windmill arrangement of arms thus simplifying register control, feeder and delivery mechanism. The ink-distribution system is of a rotary type and capable of giving complete coverage to the form.

Due to the recent acquisition of this type of platen press, it is not intended to include a chapter on operation of the press. Manuals will be procured from the company and be available to the trainee for reference.

CHAPTER 37

Concluding Remarks

The foregoing text should give the trainee the basic fundamentals of the letterpress trade as practiced in the Government Printing Office. He should, however, avoid the tendency to acquire a closed mind and become oblivious to developments in the commercial industry outside of the office. Where possible, the trainee should refer to trade publications and keep himself abreast of modern developments. He should show an interest in new equipment and methods to maintain a fresh outlook upon the trade.

The trainee can take just pride in the trade of cylinder pressman, for it is an honorable trade with a history paralleling the growth of our country. The pressman now operates presses far more complex and faster than ever thought possible. Time previously spent making ready is now spent maintaining quality throughout the run. Newer methods, better materials, and newer machines call for higher production and understanding.

The trainee should give thought to his own person and surroundings. He is potential material for supervision and the fundamentals of his trade learned at this time are most important in later years. The individual's record in the office, his character, and aptitude are examined very closely at this time and will figure very prominently in future promotions in the trade.

It will be necessary for the trainee to adjust himself to each instructor, for these men are craftsmen and recognized experts in this particular field. It will do well to admonish the trainee against criticizing the work of various pressmen. Rather he will have the unique opportunity of working with the best and observing the slovenly. Thus, he can compare and choose his way.

A healthy curiosity about the job being worked on helps maintain interest and often pays dividends that are priceless.

It is not unusual for an apprentice or trainee to initiate a suggestion that will improve efficiency and production.

The subject of good housekeeping cannot be overemphasized, for trade habits are now developing. Keeping the press and the area clean is very important to the efficiency of the individual and will be an indication of the kind of aptitude displayed.

Safety precautions not only must be observed but the trainee will have to become safety conscious. There are plenty of missing fingers about the pressroom that furnish mute evidence of disregard for safety features.

As the trainee progresses, there will be a tendency on his part to depart from the basic fundamentals as stated in this book. This is natural but he should never go so far as to prevent his returning to them.

It is absolutely necessary that he must take the initiative in a trade that is constantly changing. Twenty years ago just having the fundamentals was necessary but now the trainee will be faced with changing some of the basic concepts of letterpress work.

This text is provided as a reference to give a background, a foundation, and confidence in the trade in the years to come. Refer to it often during training and ask the instructor to clarify any part that is not understood. The instructors and supervisors will also amplify and extend the scope in any area an interest is displayed.

U.S. GOVERNMENT PRINTING OFFICE:1963

www.ingramcontent.com/pod-product-compliance
Lightning Source LLC
Chambersburg PA
CBHW081414270326
41931CB00015B/3272